MARSHALL MATHERS *In His Own Words*

Chuck Weiner

D0879819

Eminem
"*Talking*"

OMNIBUS PRESS

EMINEM *Talking*

Introduction 6

The Real Marshal Mathers 8

Who Is Slim Shady? 9

The Struggling Years 11

A Black/White Issue 14

Trailer Park Youth 21

Fighting In The Streets 25

Life & Death 27

Hip-Hop Don't Stop 29

Mommy Dearest 32

Unhappy Families 36

Mr & Mrs Mathers 37

Parenthood 40

Britney, Christina & Co 44

No Role Model 47

Friends & Rivals 48

The Music 52

Fans 74

Outrage 76

CONTENTS

EMINEM *Talking*

Therapy 78

Humour Me 79

The Media 81

Fame & Wealth 84

Influences 90

On Stage: Facing His Audience 93

Sex, Drugs, Rap'n'Roll 96

Eminem From The Outside 100

Rap Payback 107

Censorship & Taste 109

Bad Attitude 112

Who's A Faggot 116

Around The World 118

No Regrets 120

Homeboy in Detroit 123

A Regular, Ordinary Guy 126

Dre & Me 128

The Future 131

**Eminem. Marshall Mathers. Slim Shady. Is this an identity crisis
I see before me? No, just the first rap superstar of the 21st Century
who arrived late for the last one but still made a mark.**

The man who took a chocolate sweet as his rap 'tag' is no soft centre.
He was born Marshall Bruce Mathers III on October 17, 1974 and raised
on the seamy side of Detroit by his teenage mother, Debbie; he never
knew his father. Life on welfare, constantly moving home to escape the
bailiffs, was no picnic, and he found his escape route in rap and hip-
hop music, to which he was introduced by his teenage uncle Ronnie.

Introduction

School, though, was a constant trial, and at 15 one of numerous
beatings-up nearly proved fatal: a brain haemorrhage put him in a
coma for nine days. Unsurprisingly, he dropped out of the education
system after failing his ninth grade three times. The relationship with
his mother soured, his Uncle Ronnie committed suicide and Marshall
got his girlfriend Kim pregnant: what else could go wrong? (Happily,
the birth of his daughter Hailie Jade on Christmas Day 1996 was the
best moment of his life so far.)

His response to adversity was to move into music as an MC,
experiencing considerable resistance from those on the (predominantly
black) scene. Even so, he persevered, recording a now hard-to-find
first album *Infinite* for a local label. An appearance at the 1997 Rap
Olympics in Los Angeles (where, by all accounts, he was cheated of the
victor's laurels) nevertheless made a crucial connection with former
NWA man Dr Dre. The resulting album, *The Slim Shady LP*, cut in just
two weeks of studio time, would change not only his life but the face
of rap music.

But his outspoken style, voiced through his other alter ego of Shady, quickly won him many enemies. His dislike of gays attracted much critical flak, while closer to home references to his mother in the hit single 'My Name Is' led to a multi-million dollar lawsuit for defamation. Meanwhile an ongoing spat with wife Kim (which led to a summer 2000 lawsuit) also found its way into song in '97 Bonnie And Clyde'.

There was, however, an up side. *Slim Shady* won a Grammy for best rap album of 1999, and Missy Elliott, the most respected female rapper, invited Eminem to record with her – a much appreciated seal of approval. In the year 2000 he released a further album, *The Marshall Mathers LP*, which shot to the very top of the transatlantic charts. And though legal obligations following arrest on suspicion of carrying a concealed weapon prevented him from fulfilling British festival dates, a Stateside jaunt in October with Limp Bizkit, dubbed the Anger Management Tour, pulled sell out crowds and confirmed Eminem as star of the year.

By 2001, he'd added several more Grammy statuettes to a collection that now merited a trophy cabinet 'just so that Hailie can see these things when she gets older', while a high-profile performance at the awards ceremony with Sir Elton John, perhaps the world's most loved gay musician, had flipped the bird to many of his critics.

And while 2002's *The Eminem Show* exhibited a new maturity, following his escape from a prison sentence, his alliance with rap crew D12 gave him yet more licence to offend: the single 'Purple Pills' became 'Purple Hills' to avoid a radio and MTV ban. Eminem still seemed destined to have the last laugh... and his detractors the need for anger management.

INTRODUCTION

The Real Marshall Mathers

"Sometimes I'm real cool, but sometimes I could be a real asshole. I think everyone is like that."

"If people look deeper than the surface they'll discover a nice person. Only when I'm backed into a corner do I retaliate."

"I'm Marshall Mathers before I'm anything. Just a regular motherfucker that stands up for what he believes in. I'm true to my friends and family and I respect them and anyone in my circle."

"Marshall Mathers is a regular person, Eminem is a nice guy and Slim Shady is a fuckin' asshole, a complete dick. Which one do I want for a friend? Marshall. Which one do I most admire? Slim Shady. Who'd win in a fight? Slim Shady. Who's the smartest? Eminem. Who's the loser? Marshall. Who's the winner? Slim Shady."

"I wish I could come off stage and turn off the lights that flash over my head saying Slim Shady and Eminem. I wanna turn that shit off and just be Marshall Mathers again."

Who Is Slim Shady?

"I was takin' a shit. I swear to God. And the fuckin' name just popped into my head. Then I started thinkin' of twenty million things that rhymed with it."

"Slim Shady is just the evil thoughts that come into my head. Things I shouldn't be thinking about. Not to be gimmicky, but people should be able to determine when I'm serious and when I'm fuckin' around. That's why a lot of my songs are funny. I got a warped sense of humour I guess."

"I had this whole Slim Shady concept of being two different people, having two different sides of me. One of them I was trying to let go, and I looked at the mirror and smashed it. That was the whole intro of the *Slim Shady EP*. Slim Shady was coming to haunt me, was coming to haunt Eminem."

"It's just me – a different side of me, but it's not really a character. If I were to say it were a character, then it would be me slipping out of myself and being someone else. Then it would an excuse for me to go out and kill somebody – I'd be clinically insane."

EMINEM *Talking*

"I'm also in this group called the Dirty Dozen, and two or three years ago I was taking a shit and it popped in my head, because in the Dirty Dozen you have to have an alias. I'm Eminem, but in the Dirty Dozen I'm Slim Shady. I was taking a shit, thought of it, got off the pot, forgot to wipe my ass and went off to tell everybody."

"When I started using the whole Slim Shady name, it gave me the chance to take what was wrong with my life and turn it back on (to others)."

"Slim Shady is just another part of me, the dark, evil, creatively sick part."

The Struggling Years

“It was a struggle to know that I had a little girl and couldn't afford to raise her. I'm like, 'Fuck, can't afford to buy my daughter diapers.' I literally didn't have shit. So when I hit 23, that was like a wake-up point for me. Like, 'I gotta do something now.' That's when I started getting into every single battle in Detroit. It was do or die for me.”

“The first time I grabbed the mic at the Shelter (a Detroit MC club), I got dissed. I only said, like, three words, and I was already gettin' booed as soon as the mic was handed to me. I was like, 'This is fucked.' I started getting scared, like, is this gonna happen? What the fuck is gonna happen? Am I gonna make it or not?”

“I remember I used to go to this place called the Rhythm Kitchen way back in the day. I was probably 16 or 17. The first time I grabbed the mic, I got booed before I even said anything. As I started to rap, the boos just got louder and louder and louder until I just got off the mic. At this place called the Hip-Hop Shop, every Saturday, MCs would come up there and rhyme. The first time I ever got respect was the first time I grabbed the mic at the Hip-Hop Shop. I had said some shit and people was quiet at first, then cheers and applause, and it got louder and louder. That was the spot I started going to every Saturday. They'd have battles every couple of months and I kept winning them.”

“I didn't have a job that whole summer. Then we got evicted, because my friends and me were paying rent to the guy on the

EMINEM *Talking*

lease, and he screwed us over. I had to break in.
I didn't have anywhere else to go. There was no heat, no
water, no electricity. I slept on the floor, woke up, went to
LA – I was so pissed (off)."

"The Rap Olympics is usually organised so that all the entrants'
names go into a hat, and two get picked out to battle each other
with whatever comes into their head. Then the crowd decides who
the winner is, and if it's not obvious who they like best a panel of
judges decides. I went in with the mind frame that I was not gonna
lose. I needed that cash soooo bad. I had a job but I was working
part-time so I could do my rap shit. A guy came up to me
afterwards and I didn't know he was anybody from anything.
He was like, 'Yo, you got a tape or anything?' I was all pissed (off),
like, 'Yeah, here just take it.' Not knowing that he was gonna
play it for Jimmy Iovine, and Jimmy was gonna play it for Dre."

"There was this black guy sitting next to me in the crowd at the
Olympics. After the first round, he yells, 'Just give it to the white
boy. It's over. Give it to the white boy.'" MANAGER PAUL ROSENBERG

"I got with this little production company in Detroit, Web
Entertainment. I was rapping on a local radio station there, they
were like the biggest at the time when I was 15 years old, and
I used to rap on the air every Friday night with this thing called
open mic. These guys with the production team, with Web
Entertainment, I guess they heard me in their car rhyming on the
radio or whatever. They called in to the station one night, we were
talking to them. We got together, got down and then we been
working together ever since."

"We been working since I was 16 years old but I didn't have
what it took until I was 20 or 21."

"At that point in my life I had nothing. I felt like robbing somebody
or selling drugs to get myself out of the situation I was in.
I dedicated the record to all the happy people who have real nice
lives and have no idea what it's like to be broke as fuck."

A Black /
White Issue

"I was booed off stage in the early days – but I just didn't give a fuck. I started going round Detroit with MCs and winning rap competitions. I was like 'You may as will give me my respect, because I'll take it either way'. Nowadays, it's not about being black or white; if you've got the talent and somebody still tells you you can't rap, then fuck you and fuck them. Was it hard to win respect from the homies? Sure, I had to work hard to prove myself – a lot harder than the average rapper who's black. But that's only natural; rap is a predominantly black music. If I'm coming into this game, I've got to work harder if I don't want to get looked at as a joke."

"Am I white? Last time I checked I was, I guess. I looked in the mirror this morning and was combing my hair and I said, 'Wow, I'm sure white today!' I was born this way, I don't think I have much say in the matter."

"Everything is always looks. You gonna fuck with somebody – people are gonna mess with you by looks. Whether you go to a mixed school or you go to an all black school or you go to an all white school,

you gonna pick things out to mess with kids about. Growing up, that's just what you do. This kid's fat. This kid's too skinny. This kid's got buck teeth, this kid's got a big forehead – know what I'm saying?"

"I don't give a shit what people say, I am what I am. Do your fuckin' homework. I came out and people knew right off the bat I wasn't tryin' to be black. I wasn't tryin' to be anything I'm not. I was tryin' to give a reflection of my life. This is what everybody did when I was growing up; this what the fuck I'm gonna do. That 'because he's white' shit, that's a fuckin' copout to me. As much shit as I've had to fuckin' prove, I've been the underdog in this fuckin' game bein' white. I mean. I'm not stupid. I know how society is. But I've been an underdog in this game. I think I've more than proven myself time and time again. And I'm not gonna stop proving myself."

"I had to work hard and there was a certain level of respect I had to get. It was definitely an uphill battle, but I feel like I'm winning it. I'm slowly winning over the respect of everybody. I don't care if you're black, white, orange or whatever colour you are, that kid can skateboard, that kid can ride a bike, that kid can rap, that dude can play football."

"There was a while when I was feeling like, 'Damn, if I'd just been born black, I would not have to go through all this'. When you're a little kid, you don't see colour, and the fact that my friends were black never crossed my mind. It never became an issue until I started trying to rap. Then I'd notice that a lot of motherfuckers always had my back, but somebody always had to say to them, 'Why you have to stick up for the white boy?'"

"I believe that a lot of people can relate to my shit – whether white, black, it doesn't matter. I'm not alone in feeling the way I feel. Everybody has been through some shit, whether it's drastic or not so drastic. Everybody gets to the point of 'I don't give a fuck'."

A BLACK / WHITE ISSUE 99

"People (who) respect the lyrics... can look past the whole white rapper thing. I'm not the first and I'm not gonna be the last, but hip-hop music is always gonna be predominantly black. Everybody loves hip-hop but not everybody can do it. Black people started rock'n'roll, so how can anyone say that black people can't do rock'n'roll now? The world is fucked-up, it's fuckin' stupid, man. Whether you're latino, white, black, Asian, it don't matter."

"I try not to look at it that way. Being white. I don't wake up every day and look in the mirror, 'Oh. I'm white'."

"There are kids out there who, believe it or not, want to be the have-nots. The kids who come from wealthy backgrounds and listen to my music sometimes do it to say, 'Fuck you mom and dad, this is what I wanna do, I wanna listen to hip-hop and wear my hat backwards'."

"Truthfully, anything that has to do with colour, it's like, next question. You know, I don't deal with that bullshit. People are gonna say what they want to say about me and their gonna look for excuses to diss me. And that's probably gonna be one of 'em. This whole colour thing is so secondary to me."

"Unless you want to fuck me, why do you care what I look like?"

"At this point, I'm like 'Come up with something new.' I hate the same old questions. But it seems like 'white' magazines such as *Spin* and *Rolling Stone* focus on my 'whiteness' more than black magazines."

"All my life I've been dealing with my race because of where I grew up and being in the rap game. I'm at a boiling point... Anybody who pulls the race card is getting it right back in their face."

"I get offended when people say, 'So, being a white rapper... and growing up white... after being born white...' It's all I ever hear!"

"In the beginning, the majority of my shows were for all-black crowds, and people would always say, 'You're dope for a white boy,' and I'd take it as a compliment. Then, as I got older, I started to think, 'What the fuck does that mean?' Nobody asks to be born, nobody has a choice of what colour they'll be, or whether they'll be fat, skinny, anything. I had to work up to a certain level before people would even look past my colour; a lot of motherfuckers would just sit with their arms folded and be like, 'All right, what is this?' But as time went on, I started to get respect."

A BLACK / WHITE ISSUE 99

"The best thing a motherfucker ever said about me was after an open mic in Detroit about five years ago. He was like, 'I don't give a fuck if he's green, I don't give a fuck if he's orange, this motherfucker is dope!' Nobody has the right to tell me what kind of music to listen to or how to dress or how to act or how to talk; if people want to make jokes, well fuck 'em. I lived this shit, you know what I'm sayin'? And if you hear an Eminem record, you're gonna know the minute it comes on that this ain't no fluke."

"I did see where the people dissing me were coming from. But anything that happened in the past between black and white, I can't really speak on it because I wasn't there. I don't feel being born the colour I am makes me any less of a person."

"I'm not ignorant – I know how it must be when a black person goes to get a regular job in society. Music, in general, is supposed to be universal; people can listen to whatever they want and get something out of it."

"Say there's a white kid who lives in a nice home, goes to an all-white school, and is pretty much having everything handed to him on a platter. For him to pick up a rap tape is incredible to me, because what that's saying is that he's living a fantasy life of rebellion. He wants to be hard; he wants to smack motherfuckers for no reason except that the world is fucked-up; he doesn't know what to rebel against. Kids like that are just fascinated by the culture."

"They hear songs about people going through hard times and want to know what that feels like. But the same thing goes for a black person who lived in the suburbs and was catered to all his life: Tupac is a fantasy for him, too."

EMINEM WITH SNOOP DOG, DR DRE AND ICE CUBE

"Whether a white kid goes through as much shit as
I did, or didn't go through any trouble at all, if they
love the music who's to tell them what they should be listening
to? Let's say I'm a white 16-year-old and I stand in front of the
mirror and lip-synch every day like I'm Krayzie Bone – who's to
say that because I'm a certain colour I shouldn't be doing that?
And if I've got a right to buy his music and make him rich, who's
to say that I then don't have the right to rap myself?"

"Sometimes I feel rap music is the key to stopping racism.
If anything is at least going to lessen it, it's gonna be rap.
I would love it if, even for one day, you could walk through a
neighbourhood and see an Asian guy sitting on his stoop, then
you look across the street and see a black guy and a white guy
sitting on their porches, and a Mexican dude walking by. If we
could truly be multicultural, racism could be so past the point of
anybody giving a fuck; but I don't think you or me are going to
see it in our lifetimes."

"My life, my upbringing is in
the public (eye) constantly.
People know how I was
raised and whatever. So I do
black music, and there's no
escaping it, no matter how
big I get or whatever. This is
where I came from and this
is what I do, and I'm not
going to deny that.
So (nigger) is a word
I don't use by choice."

Trailer Park Youth

"I'm from the east side between Eight and Seven Mile, right where Groesbeck turns into Hoover. There used to be a Tycoon's bar and A&L Price on the corner. Street's called Dresden. That's where I grew up in. A lotta people are asking that shit, a lotta people are asking where I came from. Is his family still in the neighbourhood? Nah. My mother and my little brother are really like the only family I got. And my baby's mother and my daughter. My mother's in Kansas City right now; we have relatives back in Kansas City. We used to do a lot of moving back and forth when I was little."

"We just kept moving back and forth because my mother never had a job. We kept getting kicked out of every house we were in – six months was the longest we ever lived in a house."

"I was never into rock'n'roll, man, never. I couldn't ever tell you one rock song. My mother used to listen to it – Jimi Hendrix and shit like that. She was like a little flower child growing up in the Sixties, a little hippie."

"As soon as my mom would leave to go play bingo, I would blast the stereo."

"The worst place was a flat in a big house in Detroit that had five families living in different rooms. My mum's boyfriend's mates would all come over and go crazy. It was horrible."

EMINEM *Talking*

"I don't like to give the sob story: growing up in a single-parent home, never knew my father, my mother never worked, and when friends came over I'd hide the welfare cheese. I failed ninth grade three times, but I don't think it was necessarily 'cos I'm stupid. I didn't go to school. I couldn't deal with it."

"My life wasn't always depressed and dark. I still tend to miss certain things, like running in the streets and hanging out, shit like that. The good things were just being young and buying the hottest new albums and when I got kicked out of home, I'd be like, fuck it, and go round to Proof's. We've known each other since we were 13. We've known each other a long time. We didn't have money, but it was always liveable."

"No-one can help their colour and no one can help where they grew up, that's your parents' doing. If you grew up in the suburbs, be proud and don't pretend you came from somewhere else."

"I was born in Kansas City, and my dad left when I was five or six months old. Then when I was five we moved to a real bad part of Detroit. I was getting beat up a lot, so we moved back to KC, then back to Detroit again when I was 11. My mother couldn't afford to raise me, but then she had my little brother, so when we moved back to Michigan we were just staying wherever we could, with my grandmother or whatever family would put us up. I know my mother tried to do the best she could, but I was bounced around so much-it seemed like we moved every two or three months. I'd go to six different schools in one year."

"We were on welfare, and my mom never worked. I'm not trying to give some sob story, like, 'Oh, I've been broke all my life,' but people who know me know it's true. There were times when friends had to buy me fuckin' shoes! I was poor white trash, no glitter, no glamour, but I'm not ashamed of anything."

"As soon as I turned 15 my mother was like, 'Get a fuckin' job and help me with these bills or your ass is out.' Then she would fuckin' kick me out anyway – half the time right after she took most of my pay cheque."

"My earliest memory was raping the babysitter when I was 5... she was 15."

"My life was really shitty growing up, and obviously it influenced my music. All you got to do is pick up a *Slim Shady* album. If you listen to the album in depth, there's really not many questions to ask. I'm pretty much coming out and telling the world this is what I been through, this is what I seen, this is what I done."

"One thing I can tell you is that every single word I said about my mother and my upbringing was true."

TRAILER PARK YOUTH

"I was a smart kid, but I hated school. I just wanted to rap. I'd go to friends' houses and rap, or I'd stay in my room all day, standing by the mirror and lip-synching songs, trying on different clothes, trying to look cool."

"I was definitely different growing up, I was the distant kid. You know, real distant. The friends I did have knew me well, but I didn't have a lot of friends. I was kind of the smart ass, too. Teachers always gave me shit 'cos I never went to school. Then when I did show up, they would fuck with me. They'd be like 'Oh, Mr Mathers decided to join us today.'"

"I had a lot of full-time jobs. I had a couple of cook jobs, short-order cook and shit; factory jobs, sweeping floors and cleaning toilets and shit. Just shitty fuckin' bullshit jobs."

Fighting In The Streets

❝I was always getting jumped. On the way to school, at school, on the way back from school. I was always getting fucked with. Why? I was puny, timid. I didn't do weights until I was 17. And I lived in a fucked-up neighbourhood where there was always some kind of drama.**❞**

❝Oh yeah, one guy used to beat my ass every day. I was in fourth grade and he was in sixth, everybody was afraid of him. I was never the type to kiss ass, so he used to beat me instead. A couple of times he really fucked me up. One time he came into the bathroom and started beating me while I was taking a piss. And then, one day, him and a couple of kids ran up to me and rammed me into a snow bank, gave me cerebral concussion – I was in a coma for a week.
❝What would I do if I saw the guy now? Probably nothing. It was all a long time ago. But *Rolling Stone* magazine contacted him and he said he wanted to get in touch – he wanted them to give him my number. That motherfucker nearly killed me...❞

❝I got jumped a few times, but that happens to everybody. I don't think it has anything to do with colour or any of that shit. It's just all a part of growing up.**❞**

❝Some lady was talking shit to my mom, she came out and pointed a finger in her face, and I said, 'You ain't gonna touch my mother', so some dude comes out with a baseball bat, hit me in the stomach with it, then ran and I ended up chasing him.

EMINEM *Talking*

"While I was fighting him I had him down on the ground when the cops caught me. They didn't arrest me. I told 'em that the dude hit me first – I had witnesses and that was it. That was a long time ago."

"I used to get beat up a lot. Fights are fights. I used to walk home by myself, go to my girl's and see my friends, and when I walked back I got fucked with. It happened a lot. Nine times out of ten I would be walking by myself. Where I was growing up, everybody tried to test you."

"I've been shot at, never hit. I was 16. These gang dudes were shooting at me."

"People used to find things about me to make fun of – my hair, the way I dressed, anything. Sometimes my mother used to send me to school in these blue pyjamas. I'll never forget them. I used to roll them up in the summertime and say they were shorts. I used to get beaten up after school because of that."

"Why is it so hard for people to believe that white people are poor?! I wouldn't say I lived in a ghetto, I'd say I lived in the 'hood. The same friends I had back then are the same people on tour with me now."

Life & Death

"Uncle Ronnie was like my big brother. He knew loads about music. He became my mentor. When he died I didn't talk for days. I couldn't even go to the funeral."

"I still can't understand what happened (to Ronnie). I've been depressed and had situations when I took too many of this or too much of that, but never really wanting to kill myself. I've got a daughter and I want to look after her. I think if Ronnie had someone in his life like I have (daughter) Hailie, he would still be here today."

"I don't know whether it takes balls or it takes a fuckin' coward to kill themselves. I ain't figured it out yet. With my uncle, I just wish I could've talked to him before he did it to find out what the fuck was really on his mind."

"Suicide is always been something that's been in the back of my mind, but I don't think I have the balls to do it. There was this one time when I really felt like I wanted to do something to change my life, whether it would be doing something I regretted, or with rap or whatever."

EMINEM *Talking*

“I took a lot of them, I took a bunch of pain killers – Tylenol. I took 13, 16 of 'em and fuckin' threw 'em up. I thought I was going to die, I thought I was going to die for real.”

“We were supposed to be getting this deal from some record label – I'm not gonna say which – and we found out that this guy saying he was gonna get us the deal was working in the mail room and he was nobody. A bunch of other personal shit was happening in my life right about then, and I just thought I wasn't gonna get a deal no matter what, and I just took a fuckin' bunch of pills. I puked the shit up. I didn't have to go to hospital but my fuckin' stomach hurt so bad.

“I don't know if I was necessarily trying to kill myself, I was just really depressed and I kept thinking, more pills, more pills, I just okept taking 'em. I bet I took 20 pills in the course of two hours, Tylenol 3s. That's why I like going back and listening to my album and thinking of what I was feeling back then.”

Hip-Hop Don't Stop

"I was about nine when I started listening to rap. I started rapping, writing my own rhymes about 14 and just kept getting better.**"**

"I think it was something a little different about me; I started growing up and I just got better. At 15 or 16, I was wack. I didn't know how I wanted to sound, I didn't know anything. But at 18, 19, I started learning. This is how I should sound on the mic, learning how to battle, practising freestyle. That was what I was known for in Detroit, in the underground for a couple of years before all this happened."

"Ever since I was little kid I knew I wanted to do something, like be an entertainer, be somebody, know what I mean? The first rap record I ever heard, ever, was 'Reckless' by Ice T. I just started getting into it, breakdancing and shit like that. It just elevated from there as rap started going on. When I was like 15 or 16 I started wanting to rap. Started picking up a pencil and getting busy. I started getting better and better. Then I was like, 'Yo, I want to do this'. That's how it happened.**"**

EMINEM *Talking*

"I feel like I represent hip-hop. I've lived it all my life and I know it, I grew up on it. And I would say my sound is just pretty much for anybody who's been through some bullshit, man, who has ever been through some – trifling times or whatever. We pretty much all have, so I represent those people. All I do is reflect what's went on in my life in my music."

"For every rapper out there, hip-hop has always been known to be pretty much autobiographical. You reflect your life, you tell what you know. You say things from your point of view, like this is my point of view, this is the way I see life, it's always been like that."

"Being from Detroit and being on some different shit, I don't think it's a coincidence. You've got the East Coast and you've got the West Coast. The East Coast is predominantly known for lyrics and the West Coast is predominantly known for gangsta shit, you know what I'm sayin'? Detroit is in between both of them. So when you mix the two, you get something crazy. Kid Rock, Esham and myself are influenced by both coasts, so when you blend the two of them together you get some different shit. Which is cool. We're not supposed to sound like we're from either coast. I want my shit to sound like it's somewhere in the middle."

"Rap and hip-hop is the biggest thing, you know what I'm saying. I think rap embraces the youth, so as long as there's always youth there's always rap."

"Personally, I just think rap music is the best thing out there, period. If you look at my deck in my car radio, you're always going to find a hip-hop tape; that's all I buy, that's all I live, that's all I listen to, all I love."

"The money, the fame comes along with it, and it pays the bills, but more than anything a real MC wants to get respect. I'm sure every time Jadakiss or Jay-Z sit down with a pen and a pad, they're rappin' because they fuckin' know they're one of the best, and they want to get that respect when they write."

"I wouldn't classify my music as gangsta rap. It's not up to me to make the world kinder – I just make music."

"People reject my music for all kinds of reasons – it just gives me the fuel to make more angry music. The more people piss me off, the more I have to write about."

"Hip-hop is in my blood and I feel like I was meant to do this but, y'know, what it all boils down to is, I'm not gonna be young forever. Next in line is my daughter. She's gonna have everything when she grows up. And she's gonna be able to go to college and be something I wasn't. 'Cos if I didn't have this rap shit right now, I wouldn't have anything. I'd be a cook."

"Just know Slim Shady is hip-hop. I grew up on hip hop, it's the music I love and it's the music I respect. I respect the culture... that's me."

HIP-HOP DON'T STOP "

Mommy Dearest

❝I sheltered him too much, and I think there's a little resentment from that. People told me I'd be sorry someday.**❞**
DEBORAH MATHERS-BRIGGS

❝Ever since my success, shit hasn't been good with me and her. She wants to act like it is, and talk all this shit about, 'I love my son, and this is just a lesson that he's gotta learn. I love my son, but I'm suing him for $10 million.' In other words, 'I'm trying to take everything he's worked for away from him but I love my son.' C'mon, gimme a fuckin' break.

❝There's a lotta shit that I'm bitter for in my past that my mother has done to me that I never forgave her for 'til this day. And that's what sparked that whole thing. There's shit I'm still bitter about that she won't admit to, to my face, and all I want is an apology and I can't get it. To tell you the truth, I could never look her in the face again. For real.**❞**

"It was my mother's trailer but she wanted to move, when I got my record deal I took it over – just to give me somewhere to stay. Next thing, my mom's selling the trailer on the internet, advertising it as 'Slim Shady's trailer'. And in the paper she's saying if you buy his trailer Slim will personally come round and autograph the walls."

"My mother's crazy. She was taking my posters and shit and auctioning it off while I was on tour. She was taking posters that I'd left and selling them to the kids in the neighbourhood."

"My mother came backstage at a show in Kansas City and she was saying to the kids, 'If you want a picture with my son it's $20.' And I didn't know anything about it until this last little girl came up and said, 'Can I have my picture taken with you now cos' I've paid my $20?' My mother's a snake.

"She's mad that I said on the album that she took more dope than I do, and now she's trying to sue me for that shit. But my girlfriend talked to my mother's lawyer, who said my mother calls her every day looking for something to sue me on, and so far she has no grounds."

"I've never done drugs. Marshall was raised in a drug and alcohol-free environment." DEBORAH MATHERS-BRIGGS

"I talk to mom every now and then, but I talk to her as little as I can. She's got my little brother, so when I do talk to her, it's really to talk to him. I really don't have a reason to talk to my mother. My mother's done so much fuckin' fucked-up shit to me, now that I don't have to talk to her, I ain't gonna."

"I'm not scared of going to jail. Whatever happens, happens. Being taken away from my money, being thrown in jail, none of that shit bothers me. I'd like to watch her put herself out there and make herself look ridiculous. It's disgusting, my own mother suing me. I tell you what she's doing, she's grasping at straws."

MOMMY DEAREST

“I speak the truth, I've got no reason to fabricate my past, no reason to lie. There will be no reconciliation. I've tried, I'll say that. I can't comment further.**”**

“If my mother is fuckin' cruel enough, knowing she didn't help me get where I'm at, try to take food out of my mouth and out of my daughter's mouth, try to take me for everything that I have, then I'm not holding back on this album. She's always been out to get me, and now she knows I have money she won't leave me alone. I know that's not a nice thing to say about your mother, but unfortunately it's true.”

“She doesn't have a leg to stand on, so they're looking for things I say in new interviews which might help them, but I'm not going to give 'em anything. I would love it to go to court, I want it televised. I want people to see what type of person she is and what my life has been like. I've got no reason to fabricate my past. She could have got all that money from me anyway. I would have given it to her, but she's severed all ties by suing me.**”**

“I raised Nathan (his 14-year-old half-brother) since he was a baby. It's gonna be hard (not seeing him). When I call him I bite my tongue. I believe she's listening on the other extension. I'm sure he's afraid of my mother and I'm sure she's doing the same things to him that she did to me. When I speak to her she say's things like, 'Your grandmother is suing you now', I'm like, 'What the fuck?'”

“No, (the lawsuit is) not finished, and it probably won't be finished for a couple of years, if it even makes it to a courtroom. Of course I'm confident. Everything I said was the truth, but that's all I can say because they're looking for me to say shit now and I'm not giving it to them.**”**

Unhappy Families

"My father? I never knew him. Never even seen a picture of him. I heard he's trying to get in touch with me now. Fuck that motherfucker, man. Fuck him."

"My family has never been there for me. They expect things because we're blood."

"I had a brother and sister from his side of the family. I don't even know if he's remarried, but they knew how to reach me all this time, they knew about me. I didn't know about them. I don't know them so I can't say if they're trying to cash in on my success, but I would say that since this success, I feel like that is the reason they're trying to get in touch with me."

"Everybody in my family acts crazy about me, whenever I visit they fight over whose house I'm going to stay at. I'm like, 'What the fuck is the big deal? You guys didn't give a shit about me before, so why do you care now? Before your door was never open, now all of a sudden it's always open'."

"I've got second and third cousins coming out of the woodwork. I've got aunts and uncles crawling out of the slime, screaming they always knew I'd make it and that they'd like some money and a car. It makes me sick to the bottom of my stomach, 'cos nobody in my family ever thought I would be anything."

Mr & Mrs Mathers

❝ Just because my husband is an entertainer, that does not mean that our personal business is for everyone's entertainment purposes... I have always taken his word on things and stood by his side. **❞** KIM MATHERS

❝Nobody really knows he's married. A big part of it is that females buy 80 per cent of Marshall's records. Lots of girls are fans, and he's good-looking. They think they stand a chance. ❞ KIM MATHERS

❝ When we were younger, Kim supported everything I did. The older we got, the more reality started to set in. She's one of those people that's real down to earth, like 'Hello! You're living in fantasy. These things don't happen to people like us.' I was always the optimist, like, 'Yo, I'm gonna make this happen.' And I just kept busting my ass. To be honest, I really didn't have much support, nobody in my family, in her family. Just a few friends. And just myself. **❞**

❝Not to defend Kim, but I realise what has happened to me has probably been a strain on her, too. It's a crazy thing to deal with. You've really got to be in shape. ❞

EMINEM *Talking* **❞❞**

❝It's no secret me and the missus, we've had our problems, or that we're still having our problems. I feel like when something's bothering me, the best way to get it out is to write a song about it, I think when I do that, people can relate to me more. The more I tell them, the more in touch they are with me.

❝Because I guarantee you there's a lot of people going through this kind of shit with their relationships – with their girl, their man. I think a lot of people feel what I'm really saying. There's a lot of people out there that get in relationships and have kids involved. Once you bring a child into this world it makes it that much more complicated, especially when you don't get along with someone. You're trying to make it work, you want to make your family work. But shit keeps happening that fucks it up.❞

❝Me and Kim, we been through our dramas and shit, but I'd be bald-faced lying if I said I don't love her or I'm with her because of my daughter. I'm with her 'cos I wanna be with her. I love that girl, man. I really do. I feel like I'm starting to grow up a little bit.❞

"Does Kim trust me around other women? She don't trust me, but I try to be good. I look at like this: if I wasn't famous, girls wouldn't look at me twice. I'm not an idiot. I believe in sticking with the girl who's been with me from day one, before all this fame. Girls – not to say I hate 'em, but a lot of times they play themselves around me. You get girls who come backstage who wanna dance for me and anything just to meet me. That shit is funny to me."

"Kim thinks I'm crazy. She thinks I'm fuckin' nuts. When I did '97 Bonnie & Clyde' she was mad because I took my daughter into the studio and put her vocals on it. At the time, she was keeping me from my daughter. I barely got to see her at all. So when I did get to see her, I wanted to use that to get back at her. My daughter was being used as a weapon against me. I put the song on an EP that was only released in Detroit. I never thought it would be as big as it is. She was mad. She thinks I'm fuckin' crazy, insane for real. Maybe I am!"

"Kim used to get mad when I rapped about wanting to kill her, but I tell her: 'If you piss me off when I'm writing a song, you might be in it'. Maybe I should stop talking about my personal life, 'cos I'm ending up with no sense of privacy. But I want the fans to feel they're in touch with me."

"I've been with Kim for so long that even if we wasn't married we'd be going through the same shit. I figured I would secure the shit down at home, 'cos realistically, truthfully, that's what I need. That's the main thing that keeps my head levelled, having that security at home. I would go crazy if I came home to a house by myself."

"I've got nothing to hide. I've got a daughter, I'm proud of her. I've got a wife, I'm not so proud of her right now."

MR & MRS MATHERS "

Parenthood

❝With me not knowing my father, I try to make it up a little bit. But I don't think that's the only reason. I think parenthood comes naturally to me. I mean, I raised my little brother. My little brother was born when I was eleven years old, so I pretty much raised him from the cradle. So I think when my daughter was born, it really came naturally.❞

❝**When my daughter was born I was so scared I wouldn't be able to raise her and support her as a father should. Her first two Christmases we had nothing, but this last Christmas, when she turned three she had so many fuckin' presents under the tree, she kept opening them saying, 'This one's for me too?' My daughter wasn't born with a silver spoon in her mouth. But she's got one now!**❞

❝I'd never write a song about how much I love (my daughter). That would be like private feelings. Anyway, I don't get into all that mushy shit.❞

❝**She says, 'Daddy, you don't have to get me something everywhere we go', but I can't stop myself from spoiling her. I don't know whether it's good or bad. I'll find out when she's a teenager.**❞

"I did this so that I could be a family to Kim and Hailie and raise my daughter the right way and not cut on her like my father did to me. My family is all I have ever fought for and all I've ever tried to protect. The only thing I'm scared of is being taken away from my little girl."

"My daughter does listen to my music. She ain't really old enough to understand it now, but when she does get old enough and asks me 'What does this and this and this mean?' I'll explain it to her. I'll tell her what each thing means."

"I'm not saying that I hate kids or anything like that, but I'm not a babysitter – that's the parents' job. I listen to everything my daughter listens to and I watch everything that watches. If she watches something that has got cuss words in it she's going to hear them in school anyway, so I'd rather teach her at home that these words are bad."

"All we do as parents is contain our kids until they get into their teenage years because then you can't control them anyway. So you try and teach them not to cuss or anything but they're going to learn it regardless. Hailie listens to both of my albums and she likes them, sometimes she'll say 'Daddy put that one song on'. But she's a smart little girl and if she hears cuss words, she knows not to repeat them."

PARENTHOOD

❝I can't parent every kid in the country. Just like parents cannot prevent their kids from seeing adult films, they can't prevent them from hearing my music, I guess.❞

❝**Being a father keeps me from being too extreme. I realise that no matter how crazy I act onstage or how wild I may get, there's got to be a limit. I can't step out of a certain boundary – I have to be here for her. Her father has to remain alive. I have to maintain. She really helps me when I'm about to do something too stupid. All I have to do is think about Hailie. She keeps me in check.❞**

❝Kim looks after Hailie. Last year (1999) I was home for maybe a month out of the whole year. A month total, so I'd come home for a day, two days then go away for a week or three weeks. I got December off, but I had to record in the studio in Detroit.❞

❝**I want to try to get her into some kind of acting or something, she got this little personality that's incredible. She loves to talk. She'll say shit out of the blue, big words that I didn't even know she knew. She'll look at it as a joke.❞**

❝Much as I hate doin' the interviews and photo shoots and all the extra work that comes with the territory, that's what I'm doin' it for. So that my daughter's future is secure. So that when I die, if she never makes anything of herself – God forbid, I want her to do something, be a model, do music, be a doctor, anything – I'm ogonna have that money there for her. She'll still have that money. I want her future to be set.❞

❝**We're put here to make children. That's the reality of it. We're here to reproduce. And I reproduced. So now my life is for her.❞**

❝If I was working on something and checking out a mix, I used to play (my music) around Haile. But now I don't even want to do that any more. The more adult I'm becoming, the more I'm realising that this might have an effect on her, or it might scare her, or she might hear a word or a sentence she doesn't know how to take. With my new material, I think it's the anger in my voice even more so than the words. **"**

" Hailie knows (what I do) to some extent. I can't imagine what a 6-year-old must think... I know that she is getting some type of grasp for her father being on TV. Nobody else's dad is on TV. It must be a little head trip for her... "

" Of course you don't want your kids walking around in public going (assumes robotic voice) 'Fuck. Suck. Cunt. Ass. Bitch.' But remember how fun it was to cuss when you were in the first grade? Just to be like, 'Fuck'. 'Shit'. My little brother was three years old, running around the house saying, 'Shit. Shitty-shit. Butterfly firebutt.' It's like you can't stop it. But still, it's just words. **"**

PARENTHOOD

Britney, Christina & Co

" I don't want (to fuck) them once they turn 18. "

" I've met Britney a couple of times but I'm not going to demolish her in public. I'm not a fan of her music because I think that the boy/girl bands are garbage. I think that shit is trash, it's as corny as fuck but whatever... let them do their thing. I can't knock her for doing her thing, she sucks and she can't sing but whatever. "

BRITNEY SPEARS

" (Daughter) Hailie listens to Britney Spears and she listens to my shit too, she listens to whatever's on. My little girl watches MTV, she likes Britney Spears, Christina Aguilera and my shit. She likes a lot of people, I don't like, what am I going to do? She's four. "

" Christina Aguilera's been on MTV, talking about my personal fuckin' business. She was sittin' around with her little giggly-ass friends, they picked my video in the top ten of her favourite videos or some shit, and I had respected her until... one of the friends said (adopts high-pitched voice) 'Yeah he's cute, but isn't he married, though?' And totally blew it.

"I got married, that's my personal fuckin' business! (adopts high-pitched voice) 'I think he's married, yeah, and doesn't he have this song about killing his baby's mother and' stuffin' her in the trunk? Y'know, I always tell my friends, domestic violence and blah blah.'"

"That song was not meant to be taken seriously, that song was my sick, psychotic thoughts, 'cos she doesn't know what was goin' on in my personal life when I wrote that song, my daughter was being kept from me, but what she doesn't know, what the giggly little girl doesn't know, is that the same girl that I said I stuffed in a fuckin' trunk I married! I married her. So she was running her mouth and not knowing the fuckin' facts."

"I just find what he has to say disgusting and just completely untrue. I think it's cool of Fred (Durst) to tell the truth and not go along with what Eminem is saying, but also there is a double standard, because you see Fred playing himself in the video (for 'The Real Slim Shady'). For whatever reason, it seems (Eminem) has such animosity towards me. I don't know why. I don't know what I said to disturb him, but whatever I said I'd say again."

CHRISTINA AGUILERA

CHRISTINA AGUILERA

"Boy/girl bands, little watered-down pop groups, made bands, somebody sticks 'em together and makes something that's artificial, that's fuckin' phoney. I mean, the way that I look, people might confuse me with that. If anybody listens to my record they'll know I'm not pop, but I think it's the blonde hair thing. I just wanna make sure that people don't put me in that category 'cos every time I turn on a fuckin' TV, I'm seein' a fuckin' boy/girl group, this shit is so fuckin' corny, and it's so fuckin' commercial and fake, trash, horrible."

BRITNEY, CHRISTINA & CO

EMINEM *Talking*

JUSTIN TIMBERLAKE

"If I lose my fans 'cos they find out Eminem doesn't like NSync, I don't give a fuck. Fuck NSync, fuck Backstreet Boys, fuck Britney Spears, fuck Christina Aguilera, fuck all that bullshit, that shit is trash to me."

"I'm not mad at Backstreet Boys, or whatever – they're just doing whatever it is they do. It's not the same type of music I'm doing, so I don't feel I'm in competition with them. I think they're corny as fuck. All those boy bands and girl bands and shit. But little teenyboppers like it. So sell it and do it, I guess."

*NSYNC

"The lyrics sound like it's not a diss. It's like he likes us, but then in the video he doesn't like us." NSYNC'S LANCE BASS

"In the video, he destroys us."
JOEY FATONE

"Christina got it the worst, I feel bad for her." JUSTIN TIMBERLAKE

"I don't want to impregnate a Spice Girl any more. It's Britney Spears – she's like a green banana right now, but she'll be ripe soon."

46

No Role Model

❝I grew up listening to 2 Live Crew and NWA and I never went out and shot nobody.❞

❝I'm responsible for my little girl and that's all I give a fuck about.❞

❝It's cool (to have a) bunch of little Slim Shady (lookalike)s running around, I think it's dope. People have to remember it's just music. But I'd be lying if I said I didn't think I was a role model to kids because, whether you want to be or not, if a kid is buying your CD he is looking up to you.❞

❝My album isn't for younger kids to hear. It has an advisory sticker, and you must be eighteen to get it. That doesn't mean younger kids won't get it, but I'm not responsible for every kid out there. I'm not a role model, and I don't claim to be.❞

❝People act like Eminem is the first person to say the shit I do. Well, maybe I am the first person to say the shit to this extreme, but all I do is say what's on my fuckin' mind, man. You know, hip-hop is hip-hop and it's always been like this – from NWA to Ice-T.❞

❝I realise that there are kids buying my CDs that look up to me. But at the same time. I'm tellin' them not to do this, don't do the shit that I do. Don't copy me. I'm not trying to be a role model. I'm not trying to baby-sit kids. I got one little girl, and that's my main concern. That's who I gotta raise right; that's who I have to watch my mouth around.❞

EMINEM *Talking*

Friends & Rivals

" I like Bob, Kid Rock. He was a friend of mine. I respect what he's doing, he's being himself. I like it, but I don't listen to it every day. "

" That (first hearing ' Ice Ice Baby' in 1991) crushed me. At first, I felt like I didn't want to rap any more. I was so mad because he was making it really (hard) for me... But then (white New York duo) 3rd Bass restored some credibility, and I realised that it really depends on the individual. Vanilla Ice was just fake. 3rd Bass was real. "

KID ROCK

" There's a couple of phoney white rappers, the Insane Clown Posse – since I'm white they wanna try and take shots at me. I don't like them, cos' they're wack, and so they don't like me back. But they're fuckin' garbage. If you met them in the 'hood, would you give 'em a slap? One of them said something about my daughter, and when I see him, it'll be ugly. Very ugly. Thing is, these guys wanna battle me because I'm famous and they're not, but they're garbage – they're not even dope enough for me to respond. "

"I don't think I take the beef (with Insane Clown Posse) as seriously as they do, because I don't consider them artists. They look at me as an artist. I think they get more uptight about it. I can look at them and laugh. They can't do anything to me. What can they do to me? They have no credibility, no respect, no talent, they have nothing. All they can do is diss me vocally, they can't diss me lyrically. There's nothing they can do to me as far as the music goes. I don't take it as seriously as they do and that frustrates them."

"There's a difference between realness and an act, and Insane Clown Posse are an act, and they know they're an act, and they even say they're an act, they even say they're cornballs, they admit it."

"Will Smith don't gotta cuss in his raps to sell records, good for him. I do 'cos this is me, so fuck him and fuck you too!"

"Am I recording with Marilyn Manson? Nah, rumours, rumours."

"I heard a lot of stuff about (Lauryn Hill) and how she is toward white people and I heard she's racist. I can't prove it, but I heard a lot of stuff and there's a lot of controversy... so if she's like that I don't wanna get down like that. I don't believe in all that. That's her business if she doesn't like white people – everybody has their preferences..."

EMINEM WITH LIMP BIZKIT'S FRED DURST

FRIENDS & **RIVALS**

❝Master Ace was ahead of his time. I feel like when that album came out, I went and copped it. MC Proof was the first one who turned me on to the first album, when the second album came out, I thought it should have gone double-, triple-platinum, but it was so ahead of its time that people didn't understand. He was trying to say that hip-hop was straying from the lyrical side... like hip-hop was getting too much like 'I'll shoot you, stab you, and kill you,' and we need to get back to the lyrics.❞

❝People interviewing me over in the UK started talking about it to me and bringing it up, and it's like, 'What do you think about Elton John saying this and that about you," and I was like, "He did?' Then I read the articles where he was actually, you know, had my back on stuff, and it was cool. I was like, OK. I really respect Elton. I didn't know he was gay, I didn't know anything about his personal life, I didn't really care.❞

❝When I was 15 and Kid Rock was a couple years older, he used to always laugh and say, 'Battle me in record sales.' He saw a little bit more about the industry than I had. That's probably what I would have told somebody. No, I don't think that's what I would have told somebody. Especially back then. Back then, I was all about battling.❞

❝I hate techno music. Can I just state that for the record? I don't care who gets mad at me. I'm sorry but I just can't stand it... so no matter how good Moby is that's not gonna change.❞

❝Who the fuck are Westlife? Some boyband bullshit? I've never even heard of them. You tell me they're a pop band. Well, each to their own. Boybands are just pussies. Singing about love and shit – who cares?❞

His Part-time Rap Group D12

"The D12 record is definitely coming out along the lines of *The Marshall Mathers LP*... we have fun in the studio, and I think that's going to show. We like to clown around a lot. It's kind of my less serious side."

"We're all equal in D12. We agreed that the first one to make it would come back and get the others."

"The crew's got to stay together. You're gonna get on each other's nerves; there's gonna be fights. But we're always gonna be friends, because that's what we were before any of this shit. That's the most important thing. Just to fuckin' remember that we're friends."

"These guys haven't really got into the game yet as far as figuring out how to walk that thin line."

"We was gonna do this Western song where we were all outlaws, like the Dirty Dozen...some shit like that." EXPLAINING THE NAME

FRIENDS & **RIVALS**

The Music

"I don't try to sit down and think. I let the thoughts pop into my head, and then I write them down. I let it come natural. It's not something that I try to search for. I gotta let the stuff – throughout the course of my day, I might find six to twelve ideas. And then just jot them down and at the end of the week or the end of two weeks or whatever, I stack my ideas up and then I write a rhyme."

"**I collect ideas throughout the week. It might take a while, but I write on a sheet of paper, scattered ideas, words and metaphors. When I have enough ideas, I'll piece the shit together. When I write a full song now, I start at the corner of the paper, I write in slants. I don't know why I do that shit neither, but I do.**"

"I can't really help when the ideas come. Most of this shit comes either when I'm laying in bed waiting to sleep, or if people are talking. If they say something, a lot of the time it'll be the way people put words together, and they'll be talking to me and I won't even be listening to them because the last thing they said gave me an idea. I sit there with a blank stare and people think I'm on drugs."

"**I'm a perfectionist. I make my music for me. I know how I want it to sound. I don't think about anyone else. I listen to it and make it for me, so that I'm satisfied with it. If I am, then everybody else will like it. Usually when I write my songs, I write the verses and then sum them up with a hook. But my delivery and the way I say things across the mic, I make sure that shit is perfect, for me, so I can listen to it a million times and not find a flaw.**"

" I'm focused when I'm recording. When I record I slip into the zone. I don't like to talk a lot. I like to stick to myself and get my thoughts together, think how I'm gonna map out each song. Each song is fairly easy to write. I record vocals on one day and take the tape home to listen to them overnight. Then I do more vocals the next day.

" I always do my vocals twice. I might have the skeleton down, the vocals and the beat, for two months before I think of the finishing touches to put on it, like sound effects or if I want the beat to drop out here or something. I take my time that way. **"**

" To touch the average listener you have to use words that touch emotion. The average listener doesn't catch rhyme for rhyme and syllable for syllable. "

" I think that I've experienced a lot this year, this past year and a half, since the (*Marshall Mathers*) album came out. I think I've matured a lot and grown, which, I guess if you're a true artist, that's what you're going to do; that's what you're supposed to do. So I think people definitely hear a difference — what's the word I'm looking for? — not necessarily a different me, but a more mature (me). I think people will see my growth as far as (being) an artist. **"**

" People think it's so easy to write a rhyme or song with a catchy hook, but it's not simple. If it was the whole world would be doing it. I believe that this album will show who my true fans are, and show the people who bought my last album for 'Stan' and "The Real Slim Shady'. "

THE MUSIC

" A lot of my songs are risqué - I've been able to maintain, so far, the borderline between being cheesy and having fun and be able to come back with a serious song. There are happy sides to me just like anybody. Different moods, whatever, and that's what I try to portray. "

KIRSTEN DUNST DANCES FOR EMINEM ON 'SATURDAY NIGHT LIVE'

" My last album, *Marshall Mathers*, sold nearly two million copies in a week, which is crazy. It's a great achievement. I work hard, and it's nice to see people like my music. That's the ultimate prize for an artist. "

" I'm paranoid as fuck about anything of mine sounding like a track I just did or like anything else out there. I practically live in the studio, aside from spending time with Hailie. I always feel that I can improve something until I just get sick of it. "

"I have to tell shit like it is. What I sit around and talk about in a room with my friends – why should I not come out and say it? How would I sound talking about my theories and views and not going out and saying them in public? This is how I look at things, and if people don't like it, that's their choice. You don't have to agree with everything I say, but you put your shit out there for the world to judge."

"I still represent the underground and that class of people who can come from nothing and be something."

"In order for you to stay afloat in this business, you have to mature and you have to reinvent yourself, stay fresh. Especially with hip-hop. It's so changing forever, and it keeps elevating and going on to different levels."

"I don't know if the average listener actually sees what it is or hear the patterns and syllable rhyming and stuff like that. I don't know if they really catch that. I think they just listen and appreciate it for the beat or what it's saying. But it's a certain way that I write. Jay-Z, Nas...they crafted rhymes to the very last detail. They make it look easy so the average listener may think it's easy. But the truth is that everybody would be doing that if it was so easy."

"As an artist, you wanna keep a certain mystique. I don't ever want everybody to know everything that I'm joking about and serious about. That's the fun with creating and doing music — leaving that mystique for people's imaginations so they can get what they wanna get out of it."

"I don't feel like I've said anything different from any other rapper in the history of hip-hop. I just believe that there's a spotlight on me because I connected with those kids in those suburban homes, because I look like them and they could relate to me. I connected with those kids, and those parents got mad."

THE MUSIC

Infinite

"We put a little record out called *Infinite*. It was a little local thing. After that, we built from there. They lost money on *Infinite*, you know. They tried to put out a local tape in Detroit, it sold a little bit, but they didn't really make their money back. So, then we was getting' ready to just be like, 'Fuck it'. And then we was like, nah, there's too much there. I was like doing too many shows and getting too much response."

"I knew how to write rhymes, but couldn't really count it as a first album. It wasn't on a scale that really mattered."

"*Infinite* was me trying to figure out how I wanted my rap style to be, how I wanted to sound on the mic and present myself. It was a growing stage. I felt like *Infinite* was like a demo that just got pressed up."

"It was right before my daughter was born, so having a future for her was all I talked about. It was way hip-hopped out, like Nas or AZ – that rhyme style was real in at the time. I've always been a smart ass comedian, and that's why (*Infinite)* wasn't a good album."

"After that record, every rhyme I wrote got angrier and angrier. A lot of it was because of the feedback I got. Motherfuckers was like, 'You're a white boy, what the fuck are you rapping for? Why don't you go into rock and roll?' All that type of shit started pissing me off."

"I don't think people were ready to see a white hip-hop artist. - Producer Mark Bass on the failure of *Infinite*."

"I realise it's there, I did it, but I wasn't really experienced enough to know what to do in the studio. There was only 1,000 tapes pressed up. I think you can look it up on the internet and get it, and if you do, it'll be a bootleg."

The Slim Shady EP

❝As soon as we made the *Slim Shady EP,* we took it from there. We pressed up some little promos to give out. Then we hit Detroit with the CDs and the vinyls, and it just started picking up. We started getting orders from everywhere, I started travelling, I got on a couple of Lyricist Lounge shows... started doing shit like that. And then through the buzz, through my *Slim Shady EP*, Interscope caught wind of it.❞

❝**I had nothing to lose, but something to gain. If I made an album for me and it was to my satisfaction, then I succeeded. If I didn't, then my producers were going to give up on the whole rap thing we were doing. I made some shit that I wanted to hear. [On] *The Slim Shady EP*, I lashed out on everybody who talked shit about me.**❞

'Low Down, Dirty'
❝I was taking a shit, thought of it, got off the pot, forgot to wipe my ass and went off to tell everybody.❞

'I Just Don't Give A Fuck'
❝I'm not alone in feeling the way I feel. I believe that a lot of people can relate to my shit – whether white, black, it doesn't matter. Everybody has been through some shit, whether it's drastic or not so drastic. Everybody gets to the point of 'I don't give a fuck'.❞

'Just The Two Of Us'
❝Kim and I had broken up and were both seeing other people and she was not letting me see my daughter. My way of getting back at her was doing that song... I felt like that at the time, but now the song don't really mean shit to me.❞

The Slim Shady LP

"My album is so autobiographical that there shouldn't really be any more questions to answer. It's just the story of a white kid who grew up in a black neighbourhood who had a pretty shitty life – not the worst life in the world, but still a fairly shitty life."

"I think my first album opened a lot of doors for me to push the freedom of speech to the limit."

'My Name Is...'

"This was really simple to write. I thought of the hook right away, even before I wrote the song. Sometimes I'll do story raps and have to come back the next day to finish it. It just depends on the mood and how the shit is flowing."

"One thing I won't do is put out another song like 'My Name Is...'. I can't stand that fuckin' song. This album is rawer. Fans looking for bubblegum rap aren't going to get it here."

"Were going to sit back and listen to everything, listen to what I feel is missing on the album, if there's anything missing. I want every song to be perfect."

"'My Name Is...' blew up commercially, but we had no plans for that. We just thought it was a hot song and we put it out. Now, you've got underground kids talking shit about me like I'm a pop artist because I made one song that was catchy."

THE MUSIC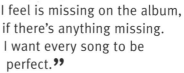

66We clicked first day in the studio, we knocked off three songs (including 'My Name Is') in six hours. Dre said he'd never done that but I was anxious to show what I could do.99

WITH DRE

'Guilty Conscience'

66Why can't people see that records can be like movies? The only difference between some of my raps and movies is that they aren't on a screen. I'm put on blast for (a rape fantasy scene in) *Guilty Conscience*, but the idea came from *Animal House*, a movie that everyone thinks is funny and wonderful. Dre and I were talking about doing a song about what's on somebody's mind when they are thinking of doing something bad, and I remember *Animal House* when the girl passes out and the guy was about to rape her. He had a devil on one shoulder and the angel on the other saying don't do it. So, we did the same thing, only a little more graphic detail.99

"When we did 'Guilty Conscience', it was pretty much Dre's concept to come up with a song with the devil on one shoulder, and the angel on the other. Dre lately has been on the positive trip, trying to clean up his image and shit. I'm at the stage where I don't give a fuck. Of course, I was the devil, he was the angel."

"I came up with the three scenarios: The liquor store, the rape, and shit. At the end of the song, I felt I was losing the battle, so I felt I had to take pokes at him. Like, 'Are you gonna listen to him?' And I remember when he slapped Dee Barnes. So when I wrote it, I didn't tell him I was going to say it. He fell over in his chair laughing, so I guess it was all good. But I was thinking the whole time, 'What is he going to say about this'?"

"The concept is from *Animal House*, where the girl is passed out and the guy has to decide what he does. He has a devil on one shoulder, an angel on the other. Movies get away with so much more than music."

'Brain Damage'

"This is a true story, except for my brain falling out of my head. I used to get harassed by these bullies in school. This one in particular, because I got a concussion and almost died. When I wrote that, I was summing up my whole years of grade school, junior high, high school. The second verse I started getting really truthful. But when I write a story, I don't want the shit to get boring, so I lay down the truth as the foundation and then mix it with a little imagination."

"Everything in the song is true: One day he came in the bathroom, I was pissing, and he beat the shit out of me. Pissed all over myself. But that's not how I got really fucked up. D'Angelo Bailey – no one called him D'Angelo – came running from across the yard and hit me so hard into this snow bank that I blacked out."

THE MUSIC

'97 Bonnie & Clyde'

"That song is a joke. Kim was trying to keep me from Hailie and this was to get back at her. It's better to say it on a record than to go out and do it."

"Look, I was pissed off! That's all I could say. I really felt that I wanted to do that shit. At one point in time, I really wanted to do that shit. For real."

"When Hailie gets old enough, I'm going to explain it to her. I'll let her know that mommy and daddy weren't getting along at the time. None of it was to be taken literally. Although, at the time, I wanted to fuckin' do it."

'If I Had' & 'Rock Bottom'

"These are a couple of the serious songs on the album. All jokes aside. Those are the songs that you can really see – I made those songs so people could really see – what I really went through, just growing up. I come from a single-parent home. Yo, we was on welfare from the day I was born. I kid you not. I never knew my father, I never knew nothing."

"These are my most personal songs but I got songs on this next album that go even deeper into that shit. I'm going a little bit more of a serious route now. My shit was real political but people didn't see it like that, they thought I was just being an asshole. I look at the way I came up and the things I was around and the places I was raised and shit, and I figure that shit made me what I am. So if people perceive me to be an asshole, the way I live made me an asshole, what I been through has made me an asshole."

"I got fired from this cooking job at Gilbert's Lodge five days before Christmas, which is Hailie's birthday. I had, like, forty dollars to get her something. That was the worst time ever. I wrote 'Rock Bottom' right after that."

"A lot of it (the album) represents my serious side. But even in the joking songs, there's still a lot of truth to the things I say. Like if I say I wanted to slit my father's throat – that's true feelings. If I say my mother does more dope than I do, that's true feelings. 'Rock Bottom' or 'If I Had'. If you listen to those, those are my two most serious songs. All jokes aside."

'Rock Bottom'

"I was like, 'I'm 23 years old, I'm not goin' to get a record deal, shit is not going to work out.' I was in the studio one night and swallowed a bunch of pills. I had to get my stomach pumped. I threw up all over my man's basement studio. The funny thing is, less than a month later Dre called..."

'As The World Turns'

"I don't think it's really politically incorrect. It's just a stupid fuckin' animated song... about being a trashy kid growing up with no morals and no fuckin' values. Every day is the same, the world keeps turnin' and I wanna get off this motherfucker. There's not even a meaning in that song. Not all songs have to have meanings to 'em. It's just funny, y'know? Laugh. Ha Ha?"

"A stupid fuckin' animated story about stereotypical white trash."

THE MUSIC

The Marshall Mathers LP

"This album's gotta anger vibe to it. It's somewhere on the edge of the sarcastic humour shit, but it's sarcasm which is too extreme to be funny. It's me backlashing at people who take everything literally. If I rap that I'm cutting my wrists, I'm just joking with motherfuckers. Do you see any wounds?

"Dre is doing a lot more than he was. He did three tracks on the last album. He's got at least seven on this one and we ain't even finished the work we're doing. Dre has been so busy with his own album. He's been mixing it down and shit, but as soon as he's finished, we're gonna start getting in there and knocking shit out like we did the last one.

"I would definitely say that the tracks I've done are killing this first album. That's the way I feel. If you don't upset the game every time you come out, if you don't make your album better than your last one, then you shouldn't even be in the game."

"People took me so serious on my last album, took me the wrong way. This album is more serious. It's also more of a feel album. You can feel these songs more than laugh at them. I say whatever I want to say, whatever is on my mind. If I get sued, if I get beat up, happens, nobody's gonna stop me saying what I wanna say. I just rock shit out. People who love me can love, and people who hate me, fuck 'em."

"I've just grown up. So maybe just for this album, I don't feel like being funny any more, know what I'm sayin? I feel like I'm dead serious this time, I'm a MC."

"My album is probably the rawest this year. It's not an egotistical assumption, that's just the way I feel. I haven't changed shit lyrically, style-wise. I'm still me. I could have made a commercial album. But I didn't. My album is underground as fuck, but the single blew up, people heard it and bought the rest of the album."

"I'm responsible for my little girl and that's all I give a fuck about."

"Don't do drugs, don't have unprotected sex, don't be violent. Leave that to me!"

"Just cos I say 'go and rape a girl' it doesn't mean do it. I'm just saying it goes on in the world."

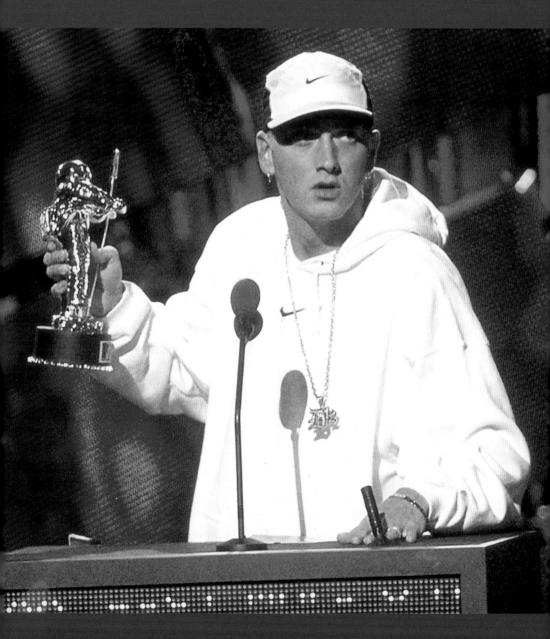

"A lot of the time, critics will take my shit out of context."

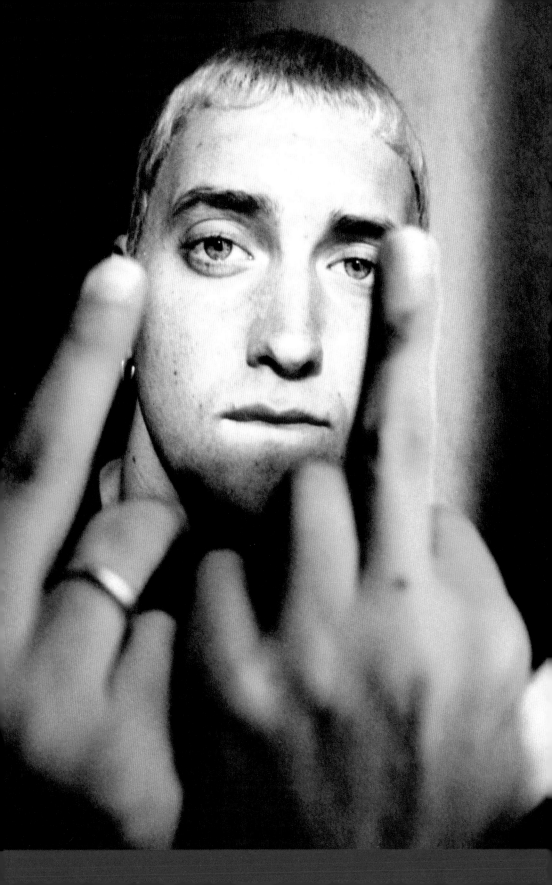

"I had a lot to say. I went through a lot in the past year so I've been building things up. On tour I couldn't really write much because we were concentrating on the shows, but when I got home in December it took me about two months to record the album."

"This album is more serious than *Slim Shady*. It's angrier, it's not as happy-go-lucky as the last album. I just reflected on things I've been through in the last year and wrote about it. People have had some things to say about me, so I've had things to say about them

"Musically, the production is better. Aside from the tracks that Dre did I've produced a few cuts myself. I produced a lot of the last record – a lot of people didn't know that. It's mostly hip-hop. One or two tracks have got some guitar, but other than that it's hip-hop and it's much rawer than the last album. I think it's better."

"I have a strategy to throw my shit out there, let people know there's something wrong with this fuckin' guy. And as soon as they hear the next album, it's gonna explain why there's something wrong (with *Slim Shady*)."

'Stan'

"Stan is suicidal and he needs someone like me to talk to. But I'm not there for him. Finally I write him a letter saying he should get counselling..."

"The song 'Stan' is about an obsessed fan who keeps writing me and tells me he's taking everything I say on the record literally. He's crazy for real and he thinks I'm crazy, but I try to help him at the end of the song. It kinda shows the real side of me."

"I wanted to make the song 'Stan' about an obsessed fan and base it on letters that I've got showing the way people perceive me. Stan is an obsessed fan who takes everything that I say and that I clown about totally serious and he just flips out. I look at almost every letter I get, but I don't have time to write back, I'm just too

THE MUSIC 99

busy. The plot is that I don't have time to write back to this guy so he thinks I'm dissing him and finally at the end of the song I write back not knowing he's killed himself. **"**

"Obviously, it's meant to be a joke but this guy was really crazy, took my music seriously and felt that he could relate to me through my music... he thought I was as crazy as he was. I attract some fuckin' weirdos... I've had dudes crying and shit. Trying to kiss my hand and looking at me like... I'm a god or something. **"**

'The Way I Am'

"When I wrote that song the label was really stressing me for a first single. I had my whole album just about finished. I went up to Interscope and played it for everybody. But everybody was saying they didn't feel like I had a leadoff single – they were all second singles, like 'Stan' and 'Criminal'. That's when I wrote 'The Way I Am', right after we had that meeting. I was feeling the frustration and pressure of like trying to top 'My Name Is'. So instead of giving them 'The Real Slim Shady' which I ended up writing at the last minute right before my deadline – thank God – I gave 'em that song. I just let it out. It was a message to the label, a message to everybody, to get off my fuckin' back. **"**

"If a critic calls me a bigot, misogynist, pig or homophobe, I'm gonna be that. If your perception of me is fucked-up, I'm gonna be fucked-up. If your perception of me is that I'm a decent guy, I'm gonna show you a decent guy. **"**

'The Real Slim Shady'

"I'm just a regular person – that's what the whole vibe of the album, that's what I'm trying to get across. Before all this rap shit, after all this rap shit, when all the glitter and glamour and all the fame is gone I'm going to go back to being Marshall Mathers. Nobody's going to give a shit about me – before they didn't. I really don't understand what the big deal is. Back home kids now look at me like I'm not a regular person, like I'm some god. They look at me crazy like I don't eat, breathe and shit the way they do. **"**

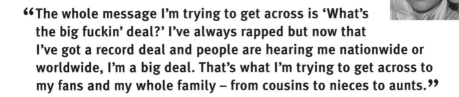

"The whole message I'm trying to get across is 'What's the big fuckin' deal?' I've always rapped but now that I've got a record deal and people are hearing me nationwide or worldwide, I'm a big deal. That's what I'm trying to get across to my fans and my whole family – from cousins to nieces to aunts."

"On one verse I was talking about a group who dissed me and made a song about me. I'm not going to say their name and give them any more light – I already gave them enough on the song. These motherfuckers dissed me, they were talking shit about me, so I let them have it. I'll let them have it in public, I'll let them have it on record, I'll let them have it verbally, physically, whatever."

'Kim'

"It's what happened before I stuffed her in the trunk. It's one big argument. I wrote that shit when I was on ecstasy. Ecstasy amplifies whatever mood you're in – love or hatred. I've wanted to kill people on ecstasy. And then I've had times when I've been telling people I don't know, I love you man!"

"It was probably the hardest song to write because it took every bit of rage that was in me to put it on paper. Like I've said before, my music is my therapy. It's the only thing that keeps me partially sane."

"She listened to it... and she was like, 'You are really fuckin' crazy'. She doesn't want to listen to the song any more. To tell you the truth, I don't really listen to the song any more. That song is like an outtake from one of our arguments in everyday life. That's really how we fight sometimes."

'Criminal'

"In the song I rap (in Southern drawl), 'Please Lord, this boy needs Jesus/Help this child, help him destroy these demons/Please send me a brand new car and a prostitute while my wife is sick in the hospital'. What I'm trying to say is we've got all these preachers going 'Jesus, Jesus!' And then they're molesting kids. I'm taking stabs at crooked motherfuckers in the system.

"When someone says kids look up to me, I'm like 'Our president smokes weed and is getting his dick sucked and is fuckin' lying about it. So don't tell me shit. I'm not the fuckin' president. I'm a rapper and I don't want to be a role model.' I'll tell a kid, 'Look up to me as someone who's come from nothing and now has everything. Don't look up to me for being violent and doing drugs. Don't be like me.'"

"It's somewhere on the edge of sarcastic humour, but it's sarcasm which is too extreme to be funny. It's me backlashing at people who take everything I say literally."

'Bonnie & Clyde Part II"

"I go through phases with my daughter's mother constantly – we've been going off and on for nine years – different phases of our relationship where I want to kill her. I don't know if you ever felt like you wanted to kill someone, but there have been times, literally, where I want to kill her. I've had songs about killing her for five years now that nobody's even heard. I've killed her, like, 11 times. The song 'Bonnie & Clyde Part II,' really 'Part I' is what happened before I killed her and stuffed her in the trunk. It's like the argument that took place. It's crazy. I don't want to give too much away. I want people to hear it. When I did it, I was kind of high, so I came back and listened to it the next day, I was just like, 'Whoa!'"

"When I went in to record that song, my daughter's mother was trying to keep her from me, and this was just a way for me to get back at her. It's better to say something like that than to actually go out and do it."

THE MUSIC

❝That song is a joke. I felt like that at the time, I wrote it to get back at Kim, but now that song really don't mean shit to me. Hailie listens to it but she doesn't understand it yet.❞

'The Showdown'
(from Wild Wild West movie soundtrack)

❝It's me and Dre. It's a Western theme. We wanted to tie in with the wild, wild West for the soundtrack. At the same time, it's a sneak preview of what's coming up on *Chronic II*. We're plugging *Chronic II* and still staying tied into the movie.❞

WITH KID ROCK

'Fuck Off'
(from Kid Rock's Devil Without A Cause)

❝We recorded our albums at the same time, in the same studio. We were even staying at the same apartments. It was a weird situation and it made us even closer… That was the very first and only time I've done coke. Made me write a song fast as hell!❞

The Eminem Show

"I think I've proven my rap skills; now I want to show that I can write whole songs, and song-songs. As far as my own solo record, my next record, it's probably going to capture a lot of emotion. I think I want to make this next record more of a feel record, where every song is different. There's emotion in every song...I want to be able to capture emotion."

"Seriously, the album sucks - please don't buy it. Just get it off the Internet like my little brother does."

"Throughout the whole album making process, only I had a copy. Nobody at the label, not Paul (Rosenberg, manager), not Proof (from D12), nobody had a copy - only me. That was premeditated and we all agreed it would be that way, just so that if anything happened I was the one to blame. That's the way we kept it locked down, which is the difference with the D12 album and my last two albums. This time, we kept this shit in my hands."

"This probably is my best album so far. This one is personal. I feel like I've grown, and in order to survive in this game I've had to grow. Everything that happens in my life I'm able to take it and write about it and reflect it. Sometimes I wonder if I need drama in my life in order to make songs and keep writing."

"I have songs on the album that I wrote when I was in that shit last year, with a possible jail sentence hangin' over my head and all the emotions going through the divorce. I went through a lot of shit that I resolved at the same time, all in the same year. And, yeah, that's when half of the album was wrote."

"If I don't show on this album that I'm a true MC then I'm quitting'"

THE MUSIC

'Squaredance'

" Can'o'shit? He's like on some fag shit. It seems like it's some queer shit to me. His little 'Stan lives', or whatever, barely peeked my radar. Hopefully he'll do something better to get my attention. No matter how big I get or whatever happens in this game, I've always got my ear to the street. If somebody – big, small, it doesn't matter - if you're an MC and you mention my name in the wrong way and you draw first blood, I'm going to come back at you. "

REFERRING TO HIS FEUD WITH RAPPER CANIBUS, WHO MOCKED EMINEM WITH HIS OWN CHARACTER STAN ON THE 'C – TRUE HOLLYWOOD STORIES' ALBUM

'Till I Collapse'

" I'll have to see what happens as far as the respect level. Yeah, I feel like I've got credit. I obviously sold records. But the things that I feel are the greatest, the rhymes that I've actually sat there and worked on for hours — I don't get recognised for them. A lot of the rhymes that I've penned in 10 minutes will get recognised, and I always sit back, like, 'That's not my favourite shit I've said'. "

'Sing For The Moment'

" (When) I thought I was goin' to jail...the scariest thought was, "How am I going to tell this to Hailie?" What am I going to say – 'Daddy's goin' away and he's bad, and you have to come visit him in jail'? I never told her anything, because if there was a slim chance that I'd get off, then I didn't want to put her through that emotionally – being scared. She hates when I go away, anytime. 'Sing For The Moment' is that frustration. "

" 'Sing for the Moment' was the first song I wrote for the album. "

'Cleaning Out My Closet'

" Honestly, there is no relationship with me and my mother. There wasn't really one to begin with, but that song is like my closure song. "

" 'Cleanin Out My Closet' was the second song I wrote for the album. I had the line – 'I'd like to welcome y'all out to The Eminem Show' – and it was just a line, but I sat back and I was like, 'My life is really like a fucking show'. "

'Hailie's Song'

" That song was stress off my chest. That's how it is with every song I do; it's therapy and it's releasing everything onto a record instead of doing any of it. I really dumped my feelings out in that song. I love my little girl enough to sing to her, for one, and two, it wasn't easy what I went through last year. "

THE ORIGINAL VERSION FEATURED RIFFS FROM GEORGE HARRISON'S 'WHILE MY GUITAR GENTLY WEEPS'

" From what I understand, he heard it before he passed and liked it. He was going to allow it. I don't understand the political side, but his wife has control of the music now, and she said no, so I had to re-sing it all and redo the song. "

About His Film, *8 Mile...*

" I always wanted to dabble but as far as taking it on first hand, it had to be a really good script. The movie is so like my life, neck and neck almost. There are differences. The script was dope enough to put my career on hold for three months... When I start slowing down with the music then maybe (I'll move into acting)... I don't think I'll ever be done with the music. This movie was like acting boot camp. "

" It's directed by Curtis Hanson, who did *LA Confidential*, so it ain't no usual gangster film that is shit. The film looks at where I grew up, and shows the story of one man's struggle to survive. I enjoyed making it and Kim Basinger, who played my mother, was dope. "

EMINEM *Talking*

Fans

"You can't control who likes you. If I got Backstreet Boy fans what am I supposed to do? Turn them away? Whoever likes my stuff likes my stuff..."

"I get a lot of fan mail, some of it's normal, and some of it's crazy fan mail. I'm a crazy guy, not clinically insane, but crazy, so I attract a lot of weirdos."

"If you speak your mind and say what you want to say, people will either love you for it or hate you for it. There's no in-between. That's what I've found just on a street level – fans, and people on the street – they either can't stand me or love me for telling the truth and saying what's on my mind."

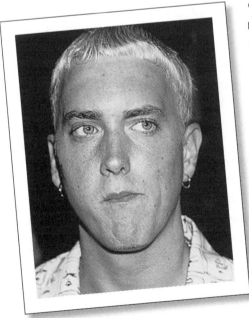

"I sometimes regret mocking my fans and my family on my records. I just wanted to make fans, regular people, feel more in touch with me, like I was a real person."

"There's kids who meet me who say they were scared to meet me, they thought I was gonna bite their head off. I'm like, Who the fuck am I? All I do is make music, and I'm doing the same thing I been doing since I was 16 years old. I ain't changed, and all these fans is kinda crazy to me."

"If I had met LL (Cool J) when I was younger I probably would have flipped out. I probably would have done what these kids do to me. I try not to be rude. I try to understand them and put myself in their position and remember what I was like at that age. But sometimes I can't help it, it gets on my fuckin' nerves."

"I attract some crazy fuckin' people. I know I ain't got it all upstairs but some people are sick. There are people who write saying they're into hurting themselves. They're cult people, fuckin' devil worshippers, who say I'm right next to Satan in their thoughts. I've had skinheads and KKK members on my case, telling me they love my shit and how I'm one of them. As a kid, much as I loved LL Cool J, Run DMC and The Beastie Boys, I wouldn't have cried, hyperventilated or had a fuckin' seizure if I met them. I'd have been real shy. Maybe even too nervous to go up and meet them."

"Motherfuckers come to my house, knocking on the door. Either they want autographs or they want to fight. We've had people getting in our backyard and swimming in our pools. I'm planning to find somewhere else to live."

FANS 99

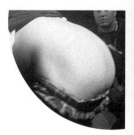

Outrage

" It's deeper than me. Oh, I want shock value, I want to shock the world. **"**

"Half of the satisfaction that I get from releasing music comes from the look on people's faces when they hear it. "

" The world is gonna get offended when they listen to my shit, and I'm so glad too. Because at the end of the day when I come out of the mic booth, I don't give a shit what I just rapped about. **"**

"I hate bitches. (One) fucked up, and it made me look at girls as sluts. "

" I pretty much say what's on my mind, but I would never say the n- (nigger) word. It's not in my vocabulary. I keep it tasteful, not like some rappers talking all sorts of shit into the microphone. **"**

"My next album is gonna be a little different, probably worse. Every time I hear critics talk shit about me, when they diss me, they only egg me on and they only make me madder. This album might have been here, but the next one will be out there somewhere. Each time I do an album, I'll just keep taking it further. "

" Yeah, I've pushed it. I can go further though, I can always go further. **"**

"I have a fairly salty relationship with women and it's always been like that. But most of the time, when I'm saying shit about women, when I'm saying 'bitches' and 'hoes', it's so ridiculous

that I'm taking the stereotypical rapper to the extreme. I don't hate women in general. They just make me mad sometimes. **"**

"I do say things I think will shock people. But I don't do things to shock people. There's absolutely nothing I wouldn't rap about. I'm a grown man and I speak my mind. I'm not trying to be the next Tupac, but I don't know how long I'm going to be on this planet. So, while I'm here, I might as well make the most of it. **"**

" My thing is this, if I'm sick enough to think it, then I'm sick enough to say it. Why are these thoughts in my head? A lot of people think shit, they just don't say it. If I'm crazy enough to think it, then I'm crazy enough to say it. That's how I base my whole shit. I think there's a reason why I think this way. I don't think I say the things I say for no reason. I write it down and say it. "

"My thoughts are so fuckin' evil when I'm writing shit. If I'm mad at my girl, I'm gonna sit down and write the most misogynistic fuckin' rhyme in the world. It's not how I feel in general, it's how I feel at that moment. Like say today, I might think something like, 'Coming through the airport sluggish, walking on crutches, hit a pregnant bitch in the stomach with luggage.'**"**

" Just cos I say 'go and rape a girl' it doesn't mean do it. I'm just saying it goes on in the world. "

OUTRAGE

Therapy

"Have I ever gone to counselling? I got a doctor for that shit.**"**

"Writing is definitely therapeutic for me. My shit is like therapy, not only when I'm writing it, but also when I'm in the booth saying it. It's a way to get shit off my chest. On my album, I've got my happy songs, crazy songs, serious songs – all jokes aside. Those are songs like, 'Okay, I've slit my wrists 90 million times, I cut my own fuckin' head off, but this is how I really feel.' I put those songs on my album so you could see for yourself. It's so clear when I'm joking and when I'm serious, but some people just don't get it."

"If people don't like my shit it's not my problem. If you don't like it don't listen to it. Nobody's fuckin' forcing you to listen to it. Nobody bought you the album, threw it in your CD, tied you up and made you listen.**"**

"My music is my psychiatrist. My microphone is my psychiatrist, it listens to me talk. Once I've got it out, I'm not mad any more."

Humour Me

"People ask me, 'Well, how do we know when you're joking and when you're serious?' 'Cos you say you don't mean everything you say, but some things you say you mean.' It's like, you don't. That's the mystique about me."

"Political incorrectness? That's just my sense of humour, man. That's how I am in everyday life. I never knew I was going to make money off of this shit."

"Some people just don't get it. Those people need more in their life than just my music, I guess."

"When NWA came out, look how literally everyone was taking it. It was entertainment and people didn't understand it. If NWA said, 'I'm gonna shoot you,' they believed: 'Oh my God, they're gonna shoot somebody.' Maybe Dre or Ice Cube was mad when they wrote that, but it doesn't mean they feel that way constantly. When I'm writing I may feel that way at the time, so I sit down and write that."

NWA

"I just take a lot of the things that are fucked up with the world and poke fun at 'em. It's like the *South Park* version of rap."

"A lot of my rhymes are just to get chuckles out of people. Anybody with half a brain is going to be able to tell when I'm joking and when I'm serious."

EMINEM *Talking*

"Anybody who took my last record seriously has got more problems than I do. How do people know what to take seriously? They don't, that's for me to know."

"A lot of the time, critics will take my shit out of context."

JOKING WITH KIRSTEN DUNST ON 'SATURDAY NIGHT LIVE'

"I think the young people are getting it. The older people are getting it confused, tending to take my shit too literal. I don't care, it's funny to me, because if I say my fuckin' brain fell out of my skull, and they believe it, what's wrong with them? The younger people have a sense of humour and can determine right from wrong. Kids are a lot smarter than we think they are. I only get flak from the white-collar motherfuckers who don't know about hip-hop anyway."

"Anybody with a sense of humour is going to put on my album and laugh from beginning to end."

The Media

❝It's funny how all the magazines can dwell on my race, but they could never say that my shit is whack because they know my shit is tight!❞

❝It's amazing that in hip-hop I'm the first motherfucker to make it outta Detroit and I gotta get hated on so fuckin' much. It's amazing. They're mad that Slim Shady fuckin' made it, that's all I can say. They're not seeing the whole fuckin' picture. If they grew up in Detroit, in the city, they would know what the fuck is going on. They would know why I feel the way I do and why I say the things I do.❞

❝Every interview I do is like, your lyrics are deadly, man, they're violent and misogynistic; or, black this, white that. But do you like the music? Is the music good? Nobody talks about that.❞

❝These British magazines and newspapers were full of shit. We performed for 40 minutes and one paper said it was only 20 and the other paper said it was 15. I only had one album's worth of material but we did two encores and performed for 40 minutes and so we did damn near every song on the fuckin' record, plus some freestyle shit and some encores. What's with your writers? Your writers are fuckin' dicks.❞

❝Why do I have to answer stupid fuckin' questions? Why can't anyone be angry any more? Which Spice Girl do I wanna impregnate? What's it like working with Dr Dre? How big is my dick? Eleven and a half centimetres.❞

EMINEM *Talking*

"I don't know which fuckin' song describes me the best! 'I Just Don't Give A Fuck', my song, describes me the best, 'cos it's about me and it's basically talking about people like you."

"I brought MTV with me; Kurt Loder came here yesterday. I took him to my old house, where new people are living at, and he brought MTV there to show where I used to live. Introduced myself to the dude. My mother was his landlord. I ain't got nothing to hide from nobody. If you wanna know and everybody in the world wants to know where I came from, then this is where I came from. And I'm gonna show you.**"**

"MTV has shown me a lotta fuckin' love, a lotta love. They really have. They've been really supportive from day one. MTV, I think, is what made radio jump on it so quickly, you know, 'cos they jumped on it. They jumped on the video before the ('My Name Is...') video was even done; when they got the rough draft of it. It's like, 'Finish it up! We wanna play it right away.' So, two days, three days later they were screening it."

"I caught more flak than any rapper I've ever seen. At first I used to get mad. Why, in every article that I read, was something about controversy, something about lyrical content? I always felt like, 'Why can't I be recognised for my talent first? When are people gonna see how crafted the music is and how much time I spend on making the music?' I used to get mad, but then I sat back like, 'You know what? Fuck it.' Maybe these people are right. Maybe I *am* terrible.**"**

Fame & Wealth

"It doesn't exactly feel like a shock, but it's all new to me, and I'm taking it in as it comes."

"I'm cool with success as long as it doesn't get too out of hand. I'm trying to keep shit balanced."

"I can (act like an asshole) on record, but out in public I can't get away with it as much as I used to. Now if I hit someone I make them rich, so if somebody gets to me physically, or there's a confrontation, I have to bite my tongue. I can't swing at that person or do what I would have done two years ago. I have people who are there for me so that doesn't happen, and to do it for me."

"I dealt with a lot of shit coming up, a lot of shit. When it's like that, you learn to live day by day. When all this (success) happened, I took a deep breath, just like, 'I did it'."

"I'd rather be asked for autographs and pictures than not, but at the same time I can't say I enjoy (fame) 24/seven. I'm not gonna lie."

"I cannot name you any entertainer I know who does not carry a fuckin' gun on them at all times. Whether it's registered, whether it's legal, whether it's not legal. It's better to be caught with it than be caught without it. I can't (carry one) no more. Just because of what's going on, you know. But entertainers gotta protect themselves."

"It makes me feel kind of sick. Some girl will be telling me how fine I am and trying to sit on my lap and I'll be thinking, 'If I was just me and I didn't have all of this fame, you wouldn't look at me twice. You wouldn't look at me once.'"

**"I don't get to see my family, my girl and my daughter. I don't get to see them. And one of the main things that's really fucked up is when people piss you off, you can't hit them in the face. We can't act like how we wanna act. How we really wanna act.
"It's really hard, man. When somebody disrespects you on a street level, you want to do something to retaliate. But you got to learn to control your temper and you got to take the 'Fuck yous' and 'You suck!' and shit like that."**

"The transition of being a regular motherfucker to now happens so fast. From the day after we shot (the 'My Name Is...') video, I remember shit moving so fast. It was like I got the Buzz Clip on MTV, then ridiculous shit just started happening. Like, I went from being home all the time to never seeing my girl to being out on the road to bitches throwing themselves at me. It was like a movie, the shit you see in movies."

"Do I want to be famous? Famous is not really the term I'm looking for. I want to be respected. I want to be looked at past the colour, past whatever fucked-up things are in people's minds, I want to be looked at past that and just be respected. But, you know, fame if it comes with it, I'm gonna take it 'cos you know, respect ain't gonna feed my daughter. Fame, money, yeah, that shit's gonna feed my daughter. But I'm in it for the long run, anyway. As long as I can do this, I'm gonna keep doing it. I ain't going nowhere."

"How is life different now? Money in my pocket, that's about it. I never stopped, nothing ever changed besides I got money in my pocket if I want something to eat. Aside from that, nothing really changed, I mean, I'm still in the studio all the time doing this rap stuff."

EMINEM *Talking*

"I don't trust nobody now because anybody I meet is meeting me as Eminem. They don't know me as Marshall Mathers, and I don't know if they are hanging out with me 'cos they like me or because I'm a celebrity or they think they can get something from me."

"The money's good, but I haven't had the time to spend much of it. The money isn't what I'm concerned with. More than anything I like what I do. I didn't start rapping because I wanted to be rich; I started out rapping because I wanted people to say I was dope. Of course I want the money, of course the money is nice, but if I'm making money and not respected then what the fuck am I doing it for? Respect means a lot to me."

"I've got a Mustang and an Explorer. I don't want a Benz, I don't wear jewellery – that's not me. This shit doesn't last forever and I don't want to wear my house around my neck or my car on my wrist. I'd rather invest and do the right things, make sure my daughter is put through college and she has an opportunity that I never had. I invest it in stocks and bonds. I've got my own record label, so I'm going to make that jump off the way that I want to."

"I could safely say that I'm well off, but I'm not a millionaire. People see me on TV and mistake me for having more money that I actually have. I got money now, more money than I've ever had in my entire life, but I still don't feel like my future is set, I still feel like I gotta work extra hard to get where I really wanna go. Shit, I still got a second album to work, possibly an acting career."

"I don't think anyone's ever caught me dressed up. I like shit that might not necessarily look good but is comfortable. Jeans and a T-shirt, that's what I'm most comfortable in, that's what I'm seen in public in."

"I'm thankful for the position I'm in, but it's got its ups and downs – being busy, not having much of a personal life, but that's the price you pay for fame and being successful. Yes in the financial sense,

no in the sense that the work's got harder, it's more of a job now
and there's a lot more to do.**"**

**"Interscope is good, the perfect label for me. I definitely
wouldn't be where I'm at today with any other label. They're a
controversial label so they're used to dealing with that.
They knew what to do and I think they marketed me the right
way, plus Dre gave me the credibility. I needed people to take me
seriously when I first came out. Before Interscope I was signed to
a smaller label. We were selling a little but we weren't selling
units, but that's how it started picking up, and the buzz we got
was from independent tapes we pressed up.**"**

"First I thought I wanted the fame, I wanted to live a better life.
But then all the kids screaming. All the girls falling at my feet. It
came so fast I didn't know what hit me. And it turned out it wasn't
even what I was looking for.**"**

FAME & **WEALTH**

"To tell you the truth, fame is not all it's cracked up to be. Fame is work, it's a lotta bullshit. My life story, my life, is like, for the public to view now. And that shit don't make me happy. It's a Catch-22, I'm thankful for every fan that I get, but on the other hand, I'm not happy, I've had to deal with racism, critics, reporters askin' stupid fuckin' questions, being too personal about my life, or my daughter, something like that. I gotta keep some sense of privacy about me. Some shit just isn't people's business."

"I went from not being able to afford nothing to limitless money, almost. I have more than I know what to do with. I can buy my daughter anything she wants, any time she wants it. And that's the best feeling in the world. That's when I realise what I'm doing all this shit for. I like the music and I have fun recording music, but I'm not selfish, if it's not making money and it's not putting food on the fuckin' table, I'm not gonna' keep doin' it for ever."

"Nothing I do is private any more. I usually feel like a monkey in a fucking cage with people looking at me. The whole *Eminem Show* concept was just, 'If the world wants a show, here the fuck it is; here's my show.'"

"There I was, in the fucking precinct getting booked, and the cops were asking me for autographs while they were fucking booking me, and I'm doing it, I'm giving them the autographs. But I'm like, 'My life is in fucking shambles right now, and you look at me like I am not a fucking person. I am a walking spectacle'."

"A lot of motherfuckers are living way better than me. Their houses make mine look like shit."

AFTER VIEWING A FEW MTV CRIBS EPISODES

"Kid Rock told me that he was getting a Presidential Rolex as a Christmas present from his label. So as a joke, I call up my label, saying, 'Yo, Kid Rock gets a fuckin' Presidential Rolex for Christmas, and all I get is a box of Interscope CDs to give to my cousins?' But I was just kidding. I don't like much flashy shit."

FAME & **WEALTH**

Influences

❝When I was nine years old, my uncle Ronnie put me on to the *Breakin'* soundtrack. The first rap song I ever heard was Ice-T, 'Reckless.' From LL to the Fat Boys, and all that shit, I was fascinated. When LL first came out with 'I'm Bad', I wanted to do it, to rhyme. Standing in front of the mirror, I wanted to be like LL.❞

❝**Tupac was good at making you feel his pain. I want to be able to make people cry, to make people feel.**❞

LL COOL J

❝Tupac had his positive songs, negative songs, angry songs, just whatever mood he was going through at the time. That's what writers do.❞

❝**I would never fuckin' put (The Beastie Boys) in a rhyme. I don't even want them wondering if I was trying to diss them. I got a lot of love for them. I grew up on that shit. The other rappers, whatever.**❞

❝When I first heard the Beasties, I didn't know they were white. I just thought it was the craziest shit I had ever heard. I was probably 12. Then I saw the video and saw that they were white, and I went, 'Wow.' I thought, 'Hey, I can do this'.❞

"The Beastie Boys were what really did it for me. I was like, 'This shit is so dope!' That's when I decided I wanted to rap. I'd hang out on the corner where kids would be rhyming, and when I tried to get in there, I'd get dissed. A little colour issue developed, and as I got old enough to hit the clubs, it got really bad. I wasn't that dope yet, but I knew I could rhyme, so I'd get on the open mics and shit, and a couple of times I was booed off the stage."

"When I was growing up, I wanted to be LL Cool J, I wanted to be Run, Ad-Rock, Big Daddy Kane, a lot of people. Me and my friends used to stand in front of the mirror and perform. The kids from the neighbourhood would come around to watch. We knew all the words."

"Tupac was at one time my favourite rapper. Tupac was more of a feel MC, a feel rapper. That's what I'm trying to do with my new shit."

"Thing is, I'm not really a commercial rapper. My whole market is through the underground; if those hip-hop heads love it, I'll rise above. It's like, you hardly ever hear a Wu-Tang song on the radio, but they rose from the underground on word of mouth."

"Growing up, I was one of the biggest fans of NWA, from putting on the sunglasses and looking in the mirror and lip-synching, to wanting to be Dr Dre, to be Ice Cube."

NWA

INFLUENCES "

❝The first hip-hop shit I ever heard was that song
'Reckless' from the *Breakin'* soundtrack; my cousin played
me the tape when I was, like, nine. There was this mixed school
I went to in fifth grade, one with lots of Asian and black kids and
everybody was into break dancing. They always had the latest rap
tapes - the Fat Boys, LL Cool J's Radio – and I thought it was the
most incredible shit I'd ever heard.**❞**

**❝Influences? I think my daughter is my main influence. When I sit
down with a pen, I mean, not necessarily influencing, but I feel
like I am doing a lot of this shit for her. I feel like if this rap
game, if this makes me the money I want to get, then I can put
her through college. But like, I don't know... influences...
I can't really say. I mean, sick shit. I don't know. I think my mind
works in a different way than a lot of other people's minds
might work.❞**

❝My room was covered in posters from *Word Up!*, *The Source*,
every rap magazine there was. You couldn't see any wall, it was
all posters. LL Cool J, Big Daddy Kane and all the rest.**❞**

On Stage: Facing His Audience

❝Some asshole kept throwing oranges and other fruit at me while I was onstage. Fucker had an arm like a major league pitcher...**❞**

❝As soon as I'd grab the mic, I'd get booed. Once motherfuckers heard me rhyme, though, they'd shut up.❞

❝Sometimes at shows, I'll pull someone on stage to battle just to make them look stupid. Some people think that I don't have it any more. 'Eminem made an album and now it's double-platinum and he can't battle no more.' That's bullshit. I do it for the fun now. I don't take it as seriously as I used to take it. Back then when I was coming up through the underground, it was a do-or-die situation. When I lost the Rap Olympics, I was ready to kill somebody. There was a $500 prize and a Rolex. I was evicted from my house and I needed that money. Now, I do it for the fun.**❞**

EMINEM *Talking*

"The worst gig I ever did was in San Francisco. These kids were fighting in the front row, and I stopped the music and told them to stop. I started the show back up and they started fighting again, so I said, 'Yo, motherfuckers, stop fighting!' and they turned to me and gave me a look like 'oh yeah – what you gonna do?' So I flew off the stage, right in the middle of them and started swinging. I got pulled down in the middle of it and these kids were stomping on me, and then my boys came running, beating the shit out of everybody. That was fucked-up shit. I thought I was gonna get arrested that night."

"I like to work for my money. I like to go out and earn crowds because it makes me feel like I'm working. Not just come out on stage and stand in one spot and the crowd just loves me the whole time just because of who I am. I want to give a show. I want to entertain people. I want to be in touch with the crowd and talk to people, keep eye contact with the people. And really just try to see what they're feeling. These are the people that's buying my records, so they're paying my way. So, you gotta keep in touch with them fans.

"If the crowd is not making no noise, I'm going to address it. Whatever the crowd is doing, I'm going to address it. If they ain't making no noise, I'm going to stop my record – 'Yo, you ain't feeling me or whatever?' If they're throwing shit and acting rowdy, I address it."

"There is usually one fuckin' heckler, or somebody who has something to say or has a fuckin' grudge and I can't react like I would normally. I usually do, but it ends up being stopped before it evolves into something ugly. But I say what I want to say, if they don't like they don't have to fuckin' listen."

"When I go out on that stage – if I'm on stage and my voice cracks or I'm losing my voice because I've been on tour for so long – if I slip and fall down and trip over a cord, whatever happens. People don't realise that whatever happens, happens. And you're just a human being. What people don't realise is that you're a regular person."

Sex, Drugs, Rap'n'Roll

"Don't do drugs, don't have unprotected sex, don't be violent. Leave that to me!"

"I had too much NyQuil and Vivarin again. Lost my stomach all over the place."

"Never take ecstasy, beer, Bacardi, weed, Pepto Bismol, Vivarin, Tums, Tagamet HB, Xanax and valium in the same day. It makes it difficult to sleep at night."

"I wasn't cute before, and suddenly girls are throwing themselves at you, literally. It was extremely fuckin' weird to me."

"Put this in bold print: I have big nuts. Huge nuts. Elephantitis of the balls, that's what I have."

"People wonder why my lyrics are so misogynistic and violent towards women, but my opinion of girls is not very high right now."

"I'm not ashamed to say I had a little pill-popping problem – just like someone else I know, who introduced me to 'em, by the way..."

"I wrote two songs for the next album on ecstasy. Shit about bouncing off walls, going straight through 'em, falling down twenty stories. Crazy. That's what we do when I'm in the studio with Dre. We get in there, get bugged out, stay in the studio for fuckin' two days. Then you're dead for three days. Then you wake up, pop the tape in, like, 'Let me see what I've done...'"

"If I'm writing rhymes I smoke weed or take Tylenol or muscle relaxants, something to get the stories rolling. Or ecstasy. Then when I'm on stage, it's Bacardi, Hennessy or ecstasy. I only do half a hit or maybe just a quarter. If I did a whole one I'd be gone. Eyes rolling, dribbling, all that shit."

"On the Slim Shady tour, I was fuckin' with that ecstasy shit every night, doing at least a hit every time. In the end, though, it gets hard on the body."

"I blacked out, had to be carried back to the hotel, then woke up with the worst headache in the world. Absinthe should mean, like, fuckin' absent in the head."

"I will be the downfall of hip hop – any rapper who hangs out with me will be addicted to drugs in a matter of days."

"I'm an attention freak. I'm only greedy when it comes to sex. I want all the women, and if I don't get 'em I fall to the ground and start kicking my feet. I'm kind of insecure about girls."

"My favourite fantasy? A bunch of girls, swinging from a nice chandelier, landing on top of me naked... while I lay in a pool of steaming hot water!"

SEX, DRUGS RAP'N'ROLL 99

❝Ecstasy is big, period – it's the drug of choice now. As soon as I stopped that I stopped fuckin' with mushrooms. You want to hear that I'm addicted to drugs, but I'm not The Red Hot Chili Peppers. I do my fair share of drugs, put it that way. I'm not saying you should or shouldn't touch anything, but have I fucked with heroin or crack lately? No, I've never fucked with that.❞

❝**What I say in my music is what I want people to know but I'm going to keep some things to myself or everybody's going to know my business.**❞

❝(Support act) The Outsidaz used to mess with girls, then they used to tell me about it. They'd say, 'Oh you want to meet Eminem? Well suck our dicks first.' It's was wild on tour with them, The Outsidaz are wild.❞

❝**The worst trouble I've been in, besides from my VD, Herpes, syphilis, AIDS. Why am I telling this? (Grins) Why do you people deserve to know this about me? I dunno if that was bad, or when I raped six 12-year old girls. Those are the top two things I've been in trouble for. I got away with all of 'em.**❞

❝A couple of the songs on the new record were written on X (ecstasy). It exaggerates shit. Somebody will be just looking at me wrong and I'll just flip a table over, like, what the fuck are you staring at? If you're in a good mood you love everybody, but if you're in a bad mood and you got shit on your mind, you're gonna break down and shit. The hardest shit that I've fucked with is X and 'shrooms.❞

"I don't fuck with coke, crack, heroin, none of the hard shit. I only did coke one time."

"I just got a tattoo of a mushroom on my arm. I had to show it off. I try not to fuck with mushrooms that much any more because that shit gets me too out of my mind. I go through phases with drugs and shit. I have a different drug of choice every other month. If I do too much of something, I say, 'I'm never doing that again!' I might stray from it for a little bit, and go back to it later. Mushrooms make me too fuckin' giggly; I just laugh at everything. I don't like to laugh too much."

On Staying Straight:

"I thought it would (affect my music) but there was a time when I thought weed and certain other drugs enhanced my writing but I learned that I can do it without. Everything that happened to me might have been a blessing in disguise."

SEX, DRUGS RAP'N'ROLL

Eminem
From The Outside

❝I liked his voice and what he was talking about. It was just different. There's no doubt people need to hear him.❞ **DR DRE**

❝He has funny songs... (but the) violence on the album isn't always funny. It depends on the way the lyrics are delivered. Some people might not be able to see the humour in the lyrics, but if they don't like it they don't have to listen to it.❞

DAVID DAVIES, WEBMASTER OF A UK EMINEM WEBSITE

❝He's changed for the worse. He talks filthy to me, and is angry and disrespectful. I don't know what's gotten into him. I will not let my grandson destroy my dead son (uncle Ronnie) with this garbage. He's a bitter boy with sad songs who wants to make fame.❞

GRANDMOTHER BETTY KRESIN

❝A friend told me, 'Debbie, he's saying this stuff for publicity.'❞

DEBORAH MATHERS-BRIGGS

❝It's some very awkward shit. It's like seeing a black guy doing country & western, know what I'm saying? I got a couple of questions from people around me. You know, 'He's got blue eyes, he's a white kid.' But I don't give a fuck if you're purple: If you can kick it, I'm working with you.❞ **DR DRE**

❝He's a suspenseful rapper... He's a star whether anyone wants to accept his lyrics or not. He's major.❞ MISSY ELLIOT

"He would come in to work and worry and say, 'The bitch took my daughter and won't let me see her. I don't know what I'm going to do. I don't know what I'm going to do'.**"** MIKE MAZUR, EMINEM'S BOSS AT GILBERT'S LODGE FROM 1993 TO 1997.

"If you're out there... living a renegade lifestyle, you might get by for a minute, but it would be a very hot minute. The pressure's on for rappers to be authentic, and Eminem might try to live up to it and get in trouble, because I know the streets are watching." WILLIE D OF THE GETO BOYS

"It was like 'White Men Can't Jump'. Everybody thought he'd be easy to beat, and they got smoked every time.**"** SCHOOLFRIEND MC PROOF

"He was no stranger to getting on mikes and getting into battles, and that's like paying your dues." LOS ANGELES RADIO DJ SWAY

"I think there's a comparison in that the same way Elvis was fusing those things, Eminem is very true to hip-hop but does bring some more rock and roll sensibility to it. It's not about him copying, it's not about imitation. It's about being inside of that enough to really incorporate it and do something different. And I think that's why people respond to it. Because in the end, Eminem is really good.**"**
SPIN MAGAZINE EDITOR ALAN LIGHT

"I love him 'cos he's white and he knows he's white. He's just him, and whatever he raps about is what he's going through. I ain't mad at that."
MISSY ELLIOT

MISSY ELLIOT

EMINEM FROM THE OUTSIDE "

"He was the one we used to pick on. There was a bunch of us that used to mess with him. You know, bully-type things. We was having fun. Sometimes he'd fight back – depended on what mood he'd be in. We flipped him right on his head at recess. When we didn't see him moving, we took off running. We lied and said he slipped on the ice. He was a wild kid, but back then we thought it was stupid. Hey, you have his phone number?" **CLASSMATE D'ANGELO BAILEY**

DR. DRE

"In my entire career in the music industry, I have never found anything from a demo tape of a CD. When Jimmy (Iovine) played this, I said, 'Find him. Now!'"

DR DRE

"When I first heard Em, I knew he could hang. The guy keeps getting more respect. (But) if it wasn't for Dre, there wouldn't be any Eminem – and vice versa." **ROBERT 'BOO' ROSARIO OF HIP-HOP MAGAZINE *THE SOURCE***

"Eminem is just incredible. I know it's what I'm supposed to say because he's with me, but this kid is really incredible.'" DR DRE

"He was a good worker, but he'd be in the back rapping all the orders, and sometimes I had to tell him to tone it down. Music was always the most important thing to him, but I never knew if he was any good at it – I listen to Greek music." **FORMER EMPLOYER AND RESTAURANT OWNER PETE KARAGIAOURIS**

"Every now and then, someone has a lightning rod right to the youth culture and this guy has it. He has an incredible ability to tell stories and if he keeps working that muscle, he could write movies, anything. He's got wit and imagination... He could write (the Marx Brothers') *A Day At The Races* if he ever wanted to."

INTERSCOPE RECORDS PROPRIETOR/PRODUCER JIMMY IOVINE

"I think a lot of people think of Eminem as a reckless, crazy, careless rapper because that's the character he plays on the record. He's lived through a lot of shit and he's had a lot of other shit thrown at him since he began selling records. But I think he's handled it well. He has fun, but he's not out of control. One thing that may help is that he never had money, so he doesn't know what the hell to do with it and he's scared to spend it. His idea of splurging is spending $500 or $600 at Nike Town." **MANAGER PAUL ROSENBERG**

"One time we came home and Kim had thrown all his clothes on the lawn – which was, like, two pairs of pants and some gym shoes. So we stayed at my grandmother's, and Em's like 'I'm leaving her; I'm never going back.' Next day, he's back with her. The love they got is so genuine, it's ridiculous. But there's always gonna be conflict there." DJ PROOF

"I wasn't worried that people would react against him because he's white. The hardest thugs I know think this white boy's tight."

DR DRE

"If he remains the same person that walked into the studio with me that first day, he will be fuckin' larger than Michael Jackson. There are a lot of ifs and buts, but my man, he's dope and very humble." DR DRE

"It's something bigger than he ever expected, the pressures that he has to go through. Just because he's doing so well, he's from Detroit, and the fact that the media keeps pointing out that he's a white rapper, it's very intense. You're talking about within a year's time going from making pizzas to being almost a household name. You can't prepare yourself for anything like this. He has to put a hat on and a hood, 'cos as soon as someone sees his blond hair they know who that is."

JEFF BASS, PRODUCER OF *THE SLIM SHADY LP*

EMINEM FROM THE OUTSIDE

"The hatred and hostility conveyed on this CD has a real effect on real people's lives as it encourages violence against gay men and lesbians. While hate crimes against gay people are on the rise, these epithets (on the album) create even more bias and intolerance toward an entire community. The real danger comes from the artist's fan base of easily-influenced adolescents, who emulate Eminem's dress, mannerisms, words and beliefs."
GAY AND LESBIAN ALLIANCE AGAINST DEFAMATION (GLAAD) STATEMENT, JUNE 2000

"Marshall Mathers had a troubled childhood, and that all comes out through the lyrics, but once he's done with that, he's Marshall Mathers, regular guy. He takes experiences from life and throws them into his lyrics and his attitude, and when it's all said and done, he's back to 'Hey, let's go get a burger.'" JEFF BASS

"I believe that a lot of these ill thoughts go through kid's minds, and I think he's made it so clear that a lot of his stuff is tongue-in-cheek. It's like he's speaking what's on people's minds, what's on his mind and whatever crazy state it's in. He's saying it in a lyrical form, expressing himself and not wishing any malice."
P DIDDY

"His content, he's gonna take you there. He definitely stepped his skills up. His album is crazy, too. It's Eminem, but he's gotten better. He's placing his words iller. His styles are iller. He's bringing skills back to the game." RAKIM

"Lyrically, he's up there with the best of them. He gets that respect. Who could say he ain't hot? I don't think anybody really wants to spar with that cat on just making a record. He has a unique style. I think he's valuable in the game." P DIDDY

"When I first heard ('97 Bonnie & Clyde'), the scariest thing to me was the realisation that people are getting into the music and grooving along to a song about a man who is butchering his wife. So half the world is dancing to this, oblivious, with blood on their sneakers.

But when you kill your wife, you don't get to control whom she becomes friends with when she's dead. She had to have a voice. **99**
TORI AMOS ON COVERING EMINEM

66 Eminem is a Caucasian male who faced criticism within the music industry that he had not suffered through difficult circumstances growing up and he was therefore a 'pretender' in the industry... Eminem used Bailey, his African-American childhood schoolmate, as a pawn in his effort to stem the tide of criticism. 99
ATTORNEY OF D'ANGELO BAILEY, SUBJECT OF 'BRAIN DAMAGE', IN PROPOSED LEGAL SUIT

66 I was inspired (to write 'The Night I Fell In Love') by all the controversy about Eminem being homophobic. I wrote it using the method Eminem uses by playing a character in the song. But I have to say we're big fans, we think he's great. **99 PET SHOP BOY NEIL TENNANT**

66 I wouldn't have (worked with him) if he was homophobic, and if he was he wouldn't have asked me. 99 ELTON JOHN

EMINEM FROM THE OUTSIDE

Rap Payback

"If somebody's got something to say about me then you best believe I am going to say something back. I'm not going to go quiet. I haven't really got into trouble for saying anything. I say whatever I want to say and whoever doesn't like it can suck my dick, and whoever likes it, cool."

"I'm gonna fuckin' dish it back to everybody who gave it to me. That's the one part that I do love about it. I sit back and wait for people to diss me. Who's the next person? And if someone does diss me I will fuckin' demolish your self esteem. I will fuckin' say everything I can in my fuckin' power to hurt you and make you wanna jump off a fuckin' bridge. I think I was given this ability to put words together like I do, in order to do this. That's how I came up, in hip-hop circles, in battles, MCing, and through arguments with my mother, fights with my girl, period. That's just how I am. I'm a very spiteful person if you do me wrong."

"I keep it gangster for everyone to see. I'm fuckin' crazy!! Yeah, I'll admit it: I'm fuckin' crazy!!! I'll kill you and you and you and you – I keep it gangster. If you don't like it, then kiss my ass!"

"A lot of the people who disrespected me are coming out of the woodwork now for collaborations. But I like doing my own shit. If there were too many other voices, the stories wouldn't go right."

EMINEM *Talking*

❝To all the people who never gave love, and continue to deny me 'cos of what I look like: suck my dick, you fucks!❞

❝**To the people I forgot, you weren't on my mind for some reason and you probably don't deserve any thanks anyway.**❞

❝I couldn't even got into a motherfuckin' club just being Eminem, before the ('My Name Is...') video. Last night they had people clearing tables for me. It's fuckin' bananas. Scary shit too, 'cos you can fall just as quick as you went to the top.❞

❝**I go back (to former workplace Gilbert's Lodge) now and pull up in a limo, just for the spite of it, hop out, go to the bar, drop a couple of hundred dollars for a tip and throw it in their faces. 'Well, Marshall, we thought you'd be blowing up by now...'. They took me for a joke, but now the joke's on them.**❞

Censorship & Taste

"A lot of parents are going to be upset and take that album right back to the store because there's nothing nice or clean about it. My lyrics are sick and there's nothing nice about them."

"I hate cleaning up lyrics for radio. I cringe every time I gotta fuckin' do it. But I got a choice. I could refuse to clean the shit up, meaning that it would never hit radio and I wouldn't have as big a voice in hip-hop as I wanna have. It's quite funny, though, singing 'chicken' instead of 'bitch'."

"Do I think my material deserves to have a parental warning on it? Yeah definitely, but it's not going to stop kids from getting it. I was 11-12 years old, listening to 2 Live Crew, sneaking into R-rated movies. Kids are kids, and kids are a lot smarter than we really give them credit for."

"The Home Secretary should ban the sale of records with lyrics like this." CONSERVATIVE MP JULIAN BRAZIER AFTER 'THE REAL SLIM SHADY' HIT THE CHARTS

EMINEM *Talking*

❝People want to try to blame
music, like the kids in
Colorado and shit like that,
people want to try and blame
the music for it, but those
kids are really crazy. It's the
music or it's the movie that
the kid's seen that made him
do it. If they want to see that
movie, they the one that did
it. Or if they want to listen
to that record, they
wouldn't of did it. Come on
man. If I'm a jump off a
bridge, I'm a jump off bridge because I want to
jump off a bridge, not because somebody told me to.❞

❝**Like any other label, Interscope runs it through a board if it's
a hot record and they look at the lyrics. Have there been times
where we had to change stuff? Yes, on both records.
Em understands that he wants the stores to stock his records or
he won't be heard, so he'll do what it takes for the most part,
unless (the complaint) is just ridiculous.**❞ MANAGER PAUL ROSENBERG

❝It's not even anything for me to get upset over. These people are
just ignorant to the music, and they don't understand. They do not
understand that damn near every song that I do has a message to
it. I'm not saying every song does, but damn near every song.
They were talking about 'Guilty Conscience' where it was me and
Dre rapping back and forth, the good half of the conscience and
the bad half of the conscience.
❝It seems that nowadays everybody's got a good half and an evil
half to 'em and it seems like the way America is now, nowadays the
bad half always rules. Evil always rules in your conscience, and
that's how crime happens. So if that little bastard couldn't see it
and see the message behind everything that I do, and analyse it –
take it lyric for lyric and see when I'm joking and when I'm not –
then fuck him.❞

"People who don't know shit about hip-hop will take it the wrong fuckin' way. It's like they refuse to see the fuckin' comedy in it. To me that shows me that I'm hitting some soft spots, for them to take my shit that seriously. It's like when they was younger they were doing this shit and they don't want to admit it now. Everybody wants to fuckin' preach, man. 'Don't do this and don't do that!' Then they go home and they do it. They say, 'Stop porn, stop porn!' Then they go home and they beat off to a fuckin' porno mag under their bed. They want everybody in the public eye to see they're so fuckin' righteous. I don't give a fuck about them."

"This man just won three major awards. Can you imagine that the entire industry honours this man who makes this despicable material? - Lynne Cheney, the wife of Republican vice-presidential candidate Dick Cheney, appearing before the Senate Commerce Committee on the tune 'Kill You'."

CENSORSHIP & **TASTE**

Bad Attitude

"When I lash out, I may be just trying to get a rise out of people or I may be expressing the way I feel. I'm in all the songs, but you might not see me at first. I think a lot of what you see in the record depends a lot on who's looking. No two people are going to see the same thing in it. I think some people get it, and some people don't have a clue. My fans get it. I don't give a fuck about anybody else."

"**There's a million of us just like me, who dress like me, walk, talk and act like me.**"

"I don't think music can make you kill or rape someone any more than a movie is going to make you do something you know is wrong, but music can give you strength. It can make a 15-year-old kid, who is being picked on by everyone and made to feel worthless, throw his middle fingers up and say, 'Fuck you, you don't know who I am.' It can help make them respect their individuality, which is what music did for me."

"**My next album is going to be a little more controversial. People already think I'm the Antichrist, so I'm at that point where if everyone's like 'You're an asshole', I'm like 'I'll show you what an asshole really is'.**"

"*Saving Private Ryan* was probably the illest, sickest movie I've ever watched, and I didn't see anybody criticising that one for violence."

"**I do promote violence and I don't give a fuck.**"

"People ask me, 'What would you say to someone that wanted to grow up to be like you?' And I would say not to do it. Don't grow up to be me. But, at the same time, is it really a bad thing to grow up to be like me, to come from the fuckin' gutter and then to become a fuckin' rap star? Is that necessarily a bad thing?"

"I remind myself of *South Park* a little bit, just the political incorrectness of it."

"I'll battle anybody who calls me out and people better know that."

"My rage comes from the anger inside me. I'm a smartass and if somebody has something to say I'm going to say something back. I can't see myself running out of shit to see. Money makes things easier but it doesn't solve your problems. You can have personal problems, you can have mental problems or problems at home and money isn't going to sort that out."

"I'd like to think I don't come across as arrogant or conceited or big-headed or anything like that. It's just me; I come across as Marshall Mathers, somebody who doesn't take shit from anybody. I don't know… I'm a real person. I answer all these questions in my music, anything that people were wondering about me. It's all there, everything that anybody needs to know about me."

"I honestly did think, once I got my record deal and shit, that I wouldn't have shit to talk about. I thought, 'What if shit is all happy? What if it is all good? And I'm not mad any more?' I feared I wouldn't have the venom and the fuckin' fire."

BAD ATTITUDE

❝It's fucked to have something that hangs over your head no matter how successful you are, no matter how far you think you've come. ... Puffy will tell you that. No matter how successful or how powerful a businessman you become, you fuck up, you're in the system. Once you're in the system, and you're fucked. Once they've got you, you're fucked. It's "Yes sir, no sir." ❞

❝**It's definitely something I regret, being in the position I'm in. It was definitely stupid. In the heat of the moment, what can you really do? You do something and you wish you could take it back, but it's done. What can you do?**❞

❝Okay, I'm a criminal and I did a couple of things that I shouldn'a did, but I'm still a human, and people make mistakes. I didn't do anything different than any other person would have done that night. Some people would have done more than me, but I don't know of a man on this fuckin' earth that would have done less – not to say exactly what I did.❞ **AFTER AVOIDING JAIL FOR PISTOL-WHIPPING A MAN HE CAUGHT KISSING HIS WIFE OUTSIDE A BAR IN JUNE 2000**

❝**I thought I was gonna go away and people was gonna forget. Some artists that go to jail, people forget about them. Their name ain't out there. Everything that you've worked for... I thought everything that I worked for could crumble, like, any day, you know? So that was nerve-racking. I'm glad to not have it hanging over my head anymore. I wash my hands of it.**❞

❝I thought I was gone for a minute. I didn't know how long, but I thought I was gone. Every day it was something. It was hanging over my head. I'm glad that it's over with, but I think that I got a lot from it and it ended up being a plus in my book. It was a reality check. It straightened me up and started making me realise, A, to calm down, and B, that this shit could all end tomorrow. My worst fear was, 'How am I gonna explain this to Hailie? What am I gonna say if I'm found guilty and I gotta do a prison sentence?'❞

What's A Faggot?

WITH ELTON JOHN

"I ain't got shit against gay people. Don't bring that shit around me and I'm cool. But they might take it, like, offensively.**"**

"Faggot to me doesn't necessarily mean gay person. Faggot to me means pussy, cissy, if you're a man, be a man, know what I'm saying, that's the worse thing you can say to a man, it's like callin' 'em a girl, whether he's gay or not. Growing up, me and my friends, faggot was a word, like 'You're bein' a fuckin' fag, man, you're bein' a fag', nobody really thought gay person, I never thought, 'You're bein' a gay person.' I don't give a shit about gay, if they wanna be then that's their fuckin' business.

"Don't try that shit on me, don't come around me with that shit but, hey, as long as they ain't hurtin' nobody, ain't hurtin' me, whatever, be gay, do your thing, if you take it in the ass, you take it in the ass, you suck dick, whatever, that's your business."

"I didn't know Elton John was gay. I just read about that recently. I respect him as an artist and musician. It's crazy, my fan base can range from five-year-old kids to 40- or 50-year-old men."

"If I said in one of my songs that my English teacher wanted to have sex with me in junior high, all I'm saying, is that I'm not gay, you know? People confuse the lyrics for me speaking my mind. I don't agree with that lifestyle, but if that lifestyle is for you, then it's your business."

"Why would it freak me out, a man suckin' another man's dick? I just said it! A man suckin' another man's dick. It's because hip-hop is all about manhood, it's about competition, about bein' macho and it just goes with the territory. I don't think people sit there and focus on it in the hip-hop community. If you're battling another dude in a freestyle battle, calling him a faggot, you're choppin' down their manhood. But I don't sit and think about it, to tell you the truth.'"

WHAT'S A FAGGOT?

Around The World

"The food in the UK is horrible, it fuckin' sucks. I don't know how you guys live. I can't see how there are fat people because I'd never want to eat. But other than that I like it, it's cool. I do think you guys are a little bit too polite, a little bit too nice."

"I like Amsterdam. But if I'm in the States or I'm in Mexico, I'm going to do my drugs regardless. It's cool that drugs are legal though. It's not cool that you can't smuggle shit out and take it home with you. What if you buy a bunch of weed and you can't smoke it all? You want to take it home with you, this shit you've paid for."

"Whenever I go to England or Germany people always ask, 'Do you like the country so far?' but I don't get to see anything. I get to see the inside of rooms, talk to people, take pictures, then do a show. So it wouldn't be a fair statement to say I don't like it. I haven't seen enough to know whether or not I like it."

"Who's Tony Blair, did he get his dick sucked? Oh he ain't shit then..."

"The show was dope! It's the first time I've been in London and I've been waiting for the moment to give some love back to all the people that have been showing me love in the UK. The shit was real! I came on thinking it was going to be a (music) industry vibe but true heads were in the crowd giving me love and it made me feel good. Like when the crowd were rapping with me – they're real fans, proving that hip-hop lives. It was off the hook, man!"

HIS FIRST LONDON PERFORMANCE AT SUBTERANEA, MARCH 1999

"London girls and Eminem just don't go together. Maybe if I could get a fuckin' girl here I wouldn't have to jack my fuckin' dick off."

"Shut your fuckin' face, Uncle Europe!"

UNBROADCAST AD-LIB WHILE IN REHEARSAL FOR *TOP OF THE POPS*

"There's a lot of places in the world that suck but I'll keep that shit confidential. There might some places that suck, but people might buy my records there."

AROUND THE WORLD 99

No Regrets?

"That's how I am. If I think something, I'll say it. Maybe I'll regret it afterwards and maybe I won't."

"I don't regret anything I've said in my songs. I really believe in that shit, man. I don't believe in talking behind nobody's back or being fake. It's fun for me to do that. When I write something I don't hold back, there's no holds barred. And whatever the consequences may be, if I offend anyone or whatever, I'm saying it so I'm willing to deal with it. I don't know if anybody does it like me, saying whatever they want to say. If I'm feeling it, then I'm gonna say it. Flat out. I'm not mad. I leave my anger in the studio. I get all my shit out on the mic, I say what the fuck I gotta say, and then I'm done. I can go home and sleep I got it all off my chest. I put it out. Music is a form of expression."

"Sometimes I feel like I'm living my life for everyone else. I wake up at seven in the morning, and the rest of the day is work. I can't sleep. I don't eat. It's just crazy. It's a lot of fuckin' work, a lot more work than I ever expected."

"Nobody really understands the pressures put on me, to always be good, to always be on point. There are so many pressures that go with my job right now. It's crazy."

"You gotta be careful what you wish for. I always wished and hoped for this. But it's almost turning into more of a nightmare than a dream. In every aspect: not being able to walk down the street any more, people not treating me like a normal human being any more. I miss going to the park and playing basketball. I was never that person who wanted big cars and Benzes. All I really wanted to do was have a career in hip-hop and be successful."

" Would I take back the last year? That's a good question. That's a real good question. It's 50-50. People would argue, 'You got everything you want. You've got money, you don't have to worry about paying bills.' But I can't even go in public any more. I've got the whole world looking at me. I can't be treated like a regular person any more.

" But there are positives, just in the sense that my little brother's not gonna need anything the rest of his life. My daughter's not gonna need anything the rest of her life. **"**

" These past couple of years have really shot by for me. Shit is speeding now. Before I was famous, when I was just working in Gilbert's Lodge, everything was moving in slow motion. **"**

" Whenever something good happens, the bad always follows. That's the story of my life since the day I was born. **"**

" My personal life is kind of fucked-up. Every aspect of my personal life is put out there. I think one of the reasons is because I make my songs for me. **"**

" Divorce was the hardest thing I've ever been through. I'm not bitter. I feel like a better person because of it. **"**

" Divorce is the hardest thing I've ever worked through – not that I'm bitter or anything like that. I'm a better person because I went through it, but it was hard at first. I've known this chick all my life, she's the first true girlfriend that I ever had. You grow up with this person, and then they want to leave you. And at first you don't know what to do. **"**

" You know, I put the blame on myself, I put the blame on my career. But as I got through it, I stepped back and looked at the whole picture. I realised it wasn't my fault and there's nothing I could have done. It was inevitable. It's cool, me and Kim are on speaking terms; we can communicate, no hard feelings, fuck it. **"**

NO REGRETS? **"**

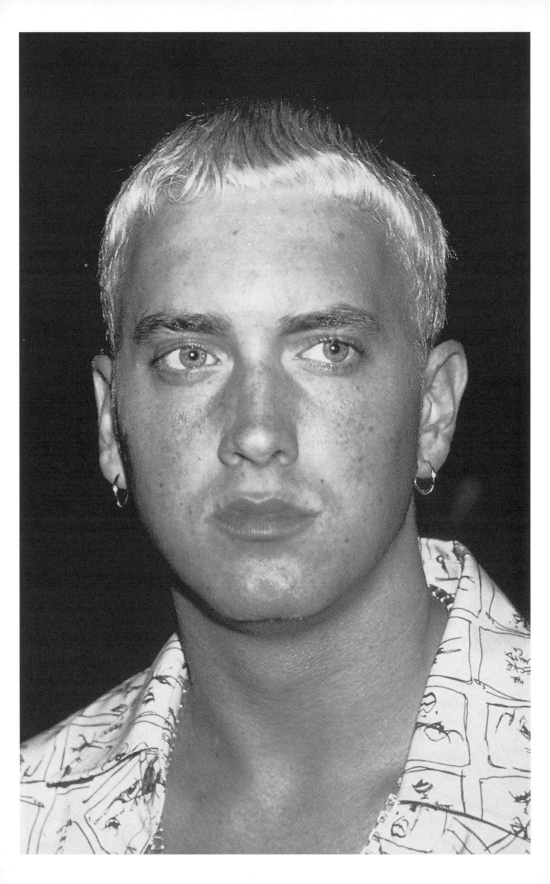

Homeboy In Detroit

"Los Angeles is a fun place to visit but I don't think I could ever leave Detroit, I got too much history there, too many roots. That's what makes it so cool about coming out here. LA is my little getaway to record my shit and then jet back home. I also got a studio in Detroit that I can go to if it's the middle of the night and I want to lay some shit down."

"About three or so years ago, not that long after my daughter was born. I was staying in this house on Seven Mile Road, and little kids used to walk down the street going, 'Look at the white baby!' Everything was 'white this, white that.' We'd be sitting on our porch, and if you were real quiet, you'd hear, 'Mumble, mumble, white, mumble, mumble, white.' Then I caught some dude breaking into my house for, like, the fifth time, and I was like, 'Yo, fuck this! It's not worth it. I'm outta here.'

"That day, I wanted to quit rap and get a house in the fuckin' suburbs. I was arguing with my girl, like, 'Can't you see they don't want us here?' I went through so many changes; I actually stopped writing for about five or six months and I was about to give everything up. I just couldn't, though. I'd keep going to the clubs and taking the abuse. But I'd come home and put a fist through the wall. If you listen to a Slim Shady record, you're going to hear all that frustration coming out."

"I lived (in the same house in Detroit) all my life, but once I hit MTV everybody was coming up to me and talking about it. People that knew me for the longest were starstruck, the kids in the neighbourhood were knocking on the door all day. It got to the

EMINEM *Talking*

point where I was like, 'I've been here all my fuckin' life, what is different about me now?' Before I could walk down the street and nobody said shit, now it's ridiculous. **"**

"Motherfuckers come to my house and violate my property, my space. If I don't know you, and my daughter's home, and I feel you're any kind of threat to me whatsoever, you're gonna get a gun in your face. That, above all, is the ultimate disrespect, to come to my door when you don't know me. "

"I stayed close to home just because I'm so used to it. Like I said, a lot of people don't understand this about me... I guess the point I'm trying to get across is not only did I never think I'd get this big, it's like I'm still refusing to believe it. I don't like having security hold my hand to walk out to my fuckin' mailbox. There's something inside of me that refuses to believe I can't walk down the street or be as normal as I want to be. That's the down side. **"**

" tried to stay close to home. For one thing I bought the house when I didn't know I would be as successful as I am now. It was like, 'I better grab this house, I don't know if any more money is coming.' I bought the house, got it on the main road ... just figuring I might get a couple of fans every once in a while. That was a big fuckin' mistake.**

"And the city won't let me put up a fence. They won't pass a city ordinance for me. They won't take my case as a special case. Everybody wants to treat me like a regular fuckin' person. But I'm not a regular fuckin' person. I've gotta have security guards sitting outside my house now because they won't let me put a fence up. The other night somebody hit one of my security guards in the head with a battery. That's they type of shit I get. "

"I like living in Detroit, making it my home. I like working out in LA, but I wouldn't want to live there. My little girl is here. **"**

A Regular, Ordinary Guy

❝I am a regular guy. Maybe I'm so successful because I am a regular person. I don't think I come across as arrogant, I come across as me, I'm myself and maybe that's why I'm successful. I am a regular person with a job, maybe with some talent but, when it comes down to it, I'm still a regular person.❞

❝I don't really read too much. It all comes from my mind and experience. Remember, I failed ninth grade three times.❞

"I do a lot of crazy shit that maybe normal people wouldn't do, but I don't know what the fuck is normal. I don't consider myself insane. I don't walk around like a fuckin' lunatic. Day to day, I consider myself pretty normal. My thoughts, what I write, I think other people think a lot of the same shit, I just think they don't say it. I may think a little bit different than the average person, but how I act, dress and carry myself, I think it's normal."

"When you don't want to sign a million autographs, when you're standing outside of your bus and you sign a few of them, then other people that didn't get their autographs are like 'fuck you, asshole!' People don't realise you're a regular person, a human being. And that's one of the hardest things that people have trouble coming to grips with."

"I don't spend much time on the Internet. I don't really get into computers and shit. I don't have the patience to sit down. I'm a jittery person; I don't like to stay in one place too long, unless I'm writing. And sometimes when I'm writing, I get up and I pace the room. Sitting at a computer, I can't really function like that. I look every now and then to see what's going on."

"I may have a better life but I know what it's like to be a regular person."

"My insecurities? I'm dumb, I'm stupid, I'm white, I'm ugly, I smell, I'm stupid and I'm white. I have freckles... um... I'm short, I'm white, I'm not very smart, I wanna kill myself. My nose is crooked. Um... my penis is small. I'm fucked."

"As a man I matured a lot, but I still like to clown and have fun. I have fun at my job. The day that I don't, I'll quit."

"I'm growing up, and I figure there's a certain level of maturity that comes with that. Hailie is better at this than I am. You know, when you build a booger castle with your daughter – that's quality time. It's actually what we live in now, and we built it ourselves."

A REGULAR, ORDINARY GUY

Dre & Me

❝Dre made me better. He showed me how to deliver rhymes over a beat, and he showed me that you stick with something until you have it just how you want it.❞

❝**Dre's the type of motherfucker that keeps is ears to the streets. He's a very humble person – he doesn't have an ego. Dre's never like, 'I'm too good to listen to this or that.'**❞

❝I just had an underground buzz – know what I'm sayin? – and he gave me credibility. People would say, 'If Dre's working with a white boy, he must be dope.'❞

❝**It was an honour to hear the words out of Dre's mouth that he liked my shit.**❞

❝I learned a lot from Dre. A lot of times I'll get a rhyme in my head and I'll know how the beats and melodies should go, so I'll go into the studio and lay it down.❞

❝**Dre is the best. The best producer of all time.**❞

❝There is a chemistry there like when Dre and Snoop Dogg first got together. It's like this – I'm a lyricist and a writer. He makes beats and produces it. He has a vision. He can make that come to life. Every Dre beat – damn near every Dre beat that I hear, I wanna rap over. It makes me instantly think of things, so like I said, it's just a chemistry. We just get together and in one studio session, we can knock out one or two songs right there.❞

"I wouldn't say I was bringing Dre back. I don't think he ever left. 'Phone Tap' on the last album, 'The Firm', was dope to me. 'Phone Tap' was one of the dopiest beats I ever heard. I just want to return the favour. Dre basically saved my life; my shit was going nowhere. Dre took me in and taught me a lot, not just rap-wise, but business-wise. Whatever I can do to return the favour, I'm here. We've got a chemistry that works and we'll make it work for however long it works.**"**

"I've been in there (for *Dr Dre 2001*) pretty much from the beginning, just being involved, giving my input, writing, doing whatever I can do to make the shit hot. The album is over-the-top, definitely some classical shit. It's going to be bigger than my album. I know this for a fact. But it's hot, man. I don't want to give any details. I just want people to be surprised. I want to sit back and say, 'I told you!'**"**

A REGULAR, ORDINARY GUY

"I would have probably quit in '97 if it weren't for Dre. My daughter was one at the time. I couldn't afford to buy her diapers. I didn't have a job. I didn't have a high school diploma, I was basically going nowhere. I was reaching a boiling point, doing a lot of drugs and fucked-up shit because I was so depressed. So when I say Dre saved my life, I mean he literally saved my life, I owe him a lot."

"Hopefully (with *The Eminem Show*) I gave Dre a break from trying to be so first-hand with my stuff. He lets me do what I want to do. Nothing I do is dope. Everything I do is not wicked and Dre will tell me. He won't sugar coat it. His honesty is one thing that I've appreciated the most, ever since he signed me."

"I can start from anything... Sometimes they'll either hit a note that will trigger a note or I'll like start a rhyme. Dre is best at seeing a vision of where the rhyme will go."

The Future

❝My main thing was I wanted to get the respect – I wanted to show the world and people who didn't believe in me that I could do this. And now that I'm doing it, I'm proving my point. And I'm going to keep proving my point until I'm tired of the rap music. I can't do it forever. You probably got about 87 more questions, you can apparently ask questions forever. I can't rap forever.❞

❝**I'm missing the best years of my little girl's life.**
I'm not seeing her grow up. There's gonna be a time
when I have to think, 'Yo, do I want this? Or do I want this?'
If I can't find a balance, I'll have to make a choice. I don't know
what's going to happen tomorrow, you know what I'm saying?
I'll have to see what happens with the next album, then I can
make a decision, but right now, I really can't.❞

❝Where do I see myself in five years? Um... 28 years old. In five years I want to be. in five years I wanna... I don't know. I want to still be rappin'. I want to keep doing this shit. I want to do it as long as I can do it. I mean, I want to do it until I can't do it any more. When I can't do it any more, I'm gonna know up in my head that I can't do it any more. Once I know in my heart that I fell off, or that I can't do it any more, then I'm gonna stop. A lot of artists, some of them just fell off, and they just keep on trying and they refuse to give up. I don't want to be one of those people...
As soon as I do that, I'm gonna quit.❞

EMINEM *Talking*

“I still got plenty of things to talk about. Just wait until the next album. I haven't thought about starting to record it yet, but let's just say that no stone ever goes unturned.”

“I've had offers to do movie roles. I haven't taken anything yet because I don't want it to take away from the music. I'm already busy as fuck. Touring, working on my new album, doing all the interviews, etc. I don't want to get too busy. I already can't see my family.**”**

“I wanna do a movie based on my life and the shit I've been through. Me and Dre have been working on this idea for a movie that, as well as my pain, is like *Saturday Night Fever* was in the Seventies and *Purple Rain* was in the Eighties. A music movie about hip-hop and the fucked-up culture of the Nineties and 2000s.”

“Everything that happens in the movie didn't necessarily happen to me. There are also going to be some things that did happen to me that aren't going to be in the movie. We're leaving the mystique, I guess.”

“I want to keep making records as long as I can, but I don't know how long you can be taken seriously in rap. There might be an age limit on it, if you know what I mean. I probably eventually will move over into producing.”

“I'm going to ride the wave however long it lasts. I can't tell you how long that will be, I might drop this album and nobody will like it. I'll still make more albums but I don't want to be rapping forever. I'm just going to keep doing it until I can do it no more.
“Then I'll take a step back and run the label, or get into production like Dre. A lot of people don't know I produce my shit. I come up with the melodies and arrangements, write all my own shit. I can't play instruments so I have these cats that play the melodies I have in my head.”

“There is a lot of different shit I want to get into. I want to branch off and do some producing of my own, I want to do some acting, I got big plans for other shit too. I want to do everything... I'm gonna be staring in some pornos. But I'm only gonna fuck fat nasty sluts. It's gonna be called *Fat Whores* and it's just gonna be different volumes of fat whores.”

THE FUTURE ”

“I'm going to be starting my own label soon called Shady Records. Right now the artist I'm looking at is MC Proof, who is on tour with me now. Actually, he's my hype man. Bizarre Kid is another MC from Detroit. It may sound biased, but I'm really trying to kick open the doors for Detroit, put Detroit on the map. I won't stop with Detroit MCs. If I come across a dope MC from another town, I'll put them on the label, but Detroit has been struggling for years.”

“I just started Shady Records with Interscope. The first signing is D12, a rap group I'm in. There's six emcees and we each have two identities, like Eminem and Slim Shady. It's not really similar to my shit. It is as far as the hard-edged rhyming goes, but if anything, it's a little grittier. I don't want to say it's underground because people associate that with shit that doesn't blow up, and I think D12's got what it takes to blow.

“It's just gritty. My shit is kind of sarcastic and political and Dirty Dozen shit is on some criminal type shit, you know what I'm sayin'? They're on some more gun-bustin' and shootin' and stabbin' shit, a little more so than I am, if you can believe that.”

“When I leave this rap game, I'm not lookin' for any of that 'He was the best', or any of that shit. I just wanna be respected.”

“I'd like to think I can keep a lengthy rap career going. But if not, I'll just go back to washing dishes.”

❝If you mean "I've sold a lot of records and now I've got a lot of money and I've made a name for myself so I should be satisfied," it's not true. Because now it's not even about the money. It's about music. If I sold 100 million records and had all the money in the world, I would still love to do what I'm doing. I still wouldn't... quit just because, OK, I'm not in this for the money and I said that in the beginning and I'll say that 'til the day I die. No matter how much money — if I succeed in this business or I don't, (if I) fail miserably — I'm still going to love to do this. If I'm recording in a big studio or I'm recording on an 8-track making demos, I'm still going to love to do this music. It's what I love the most.❞

❝You struggle all your life to get it but it's just as hard to maintain it as it is to get there. I don't ever feel I can relax and stop working. I have to keep working if I'm gonna keep being able to laugh at them people who said I wouldn't be shit or whatever. I do feel like, 'Look what I've accomplished, ha ha!'❞